Anne Griffin

Dimensions of Ethnicity

A Series of Selections from the
Harvard Encyclopedia of American Ethnic Groups

Stephan Thernstrom, *Editor*
Ann Orlov, *Managing Editor*
Oscar Handlin, *Consulting Editor*

THE AMERICAN INDIANS

EDWARD H. SPICER

The Belknap Press of
Harvard University Press
Cambridge, Massachusetts
London, England
1982

Library of Congress Cataloging in Publication Data

Spicer, Edward Holland, 1906–
    The American Indians.

    (Dimensions of ethnicity)
    Selections from the Harvard encyclopedia of American ethnic groups.
    Bibliography: p.
    1. Indians of North America.   I. Title.   II. Series.
E77.S748   306′.08997073   82–6130
ISBN 0–674–02476–1 (pbk.)   AACR2

Foreword

Ethnicity is a central theme—perhaps the central theme—of American history. From the first encounters between Englishmen and Indians at Jamestown down to today's "boat people," the interplay between peoples of differing national origins, religions, and races has shaped the character of our national life. Although scholars have long recognized this fact, in the past two decades they have paid it more heed than ever before. The result has been an explosive increase in research on America's complex ethnic mosaic. Examination of a recent bibliography of doctoral dissertations on ethnic themes written between 1899 and 1972 reveals that no less than half of them appeared in the years 1962–1972. The pace of inquiry has not slackened since then; it has accelerated.

The extraordinary proliferation of literature on ethnicity and ethnic groups made possible—and necessary—an effort to take stock. An authoritative, up-to-date synthesis of the current state of knowledge in the field was called for. The *Harvard Encyclopedia of American Ethnic Groups*, published by the Harvard University Press in 1980, is such a synthesis. It provides entries by leading scholars on the origins, history, and present situation of the more than 100 ethnic groups that make up the population of the United States, and 29 thematic essays on a wide range of ethnic topics. As one reviewer said, the volume is "a kind of *summa ethnica* of our time."

I am pleased that some of the most interesting and valuable articles in the encyclopedia are now available to a wider audience through inexpensive paperback editions such as this one. These essays will be an excellent starting point for anyone in search of deeper understanding of who the American people are and how they came to be that way.

Stephan Thernstrom

Contents

The American Indians

In the 1970s there were 173 American Indian groups, variously called tribes, nations, bands, peoples, and ethnic groups. The largest of these—the Navajos of Arizona and New Mexico—numbered more than 160,000, the smallest—such as the Chumash of California and the Modocs of Oklahoma—fewer than a hundred. Nearly as many Indian tribes exist in the 20th century as when Europeans first encountered them in the 1600s.

It is not known precisely how many different nations (as they were then called by Europeans) existed at the time of first contact. A widely accepted rough estimate is that there were, in the late 1600s, upward of 200. If so, it can be said that the number of groups has declined by only about 30, or perhaps 16 percent. But these figures do not tell the whole story. Fifty or more groups are known to have become extinct as a result of disease, massacre by whites, absorption into other groups, or harsh conditions during the early phase of contact with Europeans. It is safe to say that one-fourth suffered extinction.

On the other hand, groups with a new sense of identity have been formed as a result of nations being separated into two or more groups and having different experiences in the course of their later history. The Cherokees of Oklahoma and the Eastern Band of Cherokees in North Carolina, the Citizen Potawatomis of Oklahoma and the Forest Potawatomis of Michigan are two of many examples. Also several remnant groups have sometimes consolidated into a single new one, such as the Brothertons and the Stockbridge Indians, once of

New Jersey and New England, respectively, and now of Michigan.

The important fact is that American Indians have maintained a high degree of diversity and continue to develop in a variety of ways. They were not and have not become a single undifferentiated people justifying the single label—the American Indian—as most Americans believe. They comprise at least 170 peoples with different cultural backgrounds, different historical experiences, and, as a result, different senses of identity.

Nor are Indians, as popular belief portrays them, a vanishing people. Expert estimates of precisely how many Indians there were within the territory of the United States when the white man arrived range from a conservative and widely accepted figure of 850,000 up to more than a million. The United States Census count for 1970 was 791,839. Although this suggests a decline in population, if we look more deeply into the figures, a different view emerges. The Indian population did indeed decline rapidly from the 1600s through the 1800s. In 1900 it was recorded as 237,196, indicating a nearly 75 percent decline during the previous 200 years. The greatest reduction took place during the 19th century, and undoubtedly it is that period of deep decline that gave rise to the stereotype of the Indians as a vanishing race.

However, from 1900 the trend has been toward a continuing increase, especially in the 20-year period from 1950 to 1970, when there was an increase of 100 percent. It appears that the Indian population in the 1980s will considerably exceed what it was in the early years of European contact.

In respect to both numbers of individuals and numbers of distinct ethnic groups, Indians have held their own over the past 300 years, and recently the rate of growth has accelerated greatly. These facts are significant for understanding the place of Indians in the American system of ethnic relations, as is their distribution in the general population and the historical events that account for that distribution.

Nearly 700,000 Indians—the overwhelming majority—

live west of the Mississippi River. In 1970 almost half of this population lived in three western states: Oklahoma, with 97,731; Arizona, with 95,812; and California, with 91,018. In contrast, 25 states east of the Mississippi (not including Michigan and Wisconsin) had an Indian population of only 128,525, or about one-fifth of the total (see Fig. 1).

These figures reflect fairly closely the historical circumstances that have powerfully affected Indian life during the past two centuries. To some extent the relatively small number of Indians throughout the East is a result of early decimation by disease (which hit Indians hardest during their initial European contacts), warfare, and massacre. However, the primary cause for depopulation was the government policy of systematically forced migration, as white Americans put heavy pressure on Indians to move out of their way, that is, westward. They usually paid something for Indian land but forced the sale whenever Indians were slow or refused to move. The most extensive program of removal and deportation began about 1830, when the Five Civilized Tribes—to be defined later—of the Southeast were forced into agreements to move to Indian Territory. At least 70,000, of whom some 20,000 died en route, were thus removed from the southeastern states. Similarly, the Indians of the Ohio Valley were pushed west, leaving some of the best farmland in the United States. By the late 1800s only tiny Indian enclaves remained east of the Mississippi, such as the Wampanoags in Massachusetts and the Catawbas in South Carolina, except for a few larger remaining groups: in New York, where most of the Iroquois somehow withstood the pressures; in the states bordering the three western Great Lakes; and in North Carolina, where unusual circumstances resulted in the creation of an entirely new tribe of 40,000—the Lumbees.

The present concentration of the Indian population in three western states also reflects important historical developments. Oklahoma, with the largest Indian population in 1970, was once Indian Territory, to which the Five Civilized Tribes were deported, as were many other eastern, midwest-

A Warm Springs Reservation
Chetco   Umpqua
Coos Bay   Wasco
Cowlitz   Weaco
Klickitat   Wishram
Siuslaw   Yakima-Klickitat
Tenino

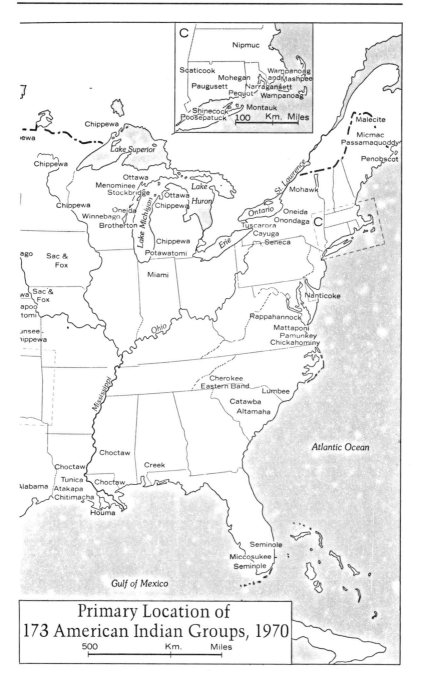

Primary Location of
173 American Indian Groups, 1970

ern, and Plains tribes. Oklahoma represents the major monument to the removal policy.

The second-largest concentration of Indian population is in Arizona, for quite different reasons. First, the Pueblos and the Piman-speaking peoples, who were already settled as farmers there when the Spaniards began their colonization from New Spain in 1598, were not removed from their lands by either Spanish or American conquerors, although there was much encroachment by whites. However, the high population figure in the Arizona–New Mexico region is mainly a result of the spectacular growth of the Navajo Indians, who in Arizona, New Mexico, and Utah came to occupy the largest of all Indian reservations. They increased from fewer than 9,000 during early Spanish colonization to more than 160,000 in 1975, becoming the largest Indian nation in the United States. Their relative freedom to develop in their own way as sheepherders in sparsely settled country for most of a century (between 1868 and the 1930s), with little or no government interference, played a part in their population explosion. In the Southwest, then, a considerable segment of Indian population has experienced a minimum of dislocation, has expanded in numbers, and has developed distinctive ways of life.

The third-largest Indian concentration is in California. Although some portion of this population consists of rural native California Indians for whom federal reserves were never created, by far the greater part is the result of large-scale voluntary migration from reservations to San Francisco and the Bay region, Los Angeles, and San Diego during and after World War II.

Thus the present distribution of Indians reflects the forced migrations of the 19th century, the relative isolation of some groups, especially in the West, and the more recent migration from the rural reservations to the cities.

During the early period of European settlement, Indians were distributed in a very different pattern across the continent. The East was more heavily populated over most of its breadth than was the West. There were also areas of relatively high density: for example, southern New England, where the Massachusetts and Connecticut Indians lived; tidewater Virginia, where the Powhatan Confederacy arose; and the coastal areas of the Carolinas. Other relatively dense populations existed in the country of the Choctaws, Creeks, and Cherokees. All these areas were almost devoid of Indians by the 19th century. In the vast expanse of the West, which was relatively sparsely populated by Indians, there were also areas of higher density: the Southwest Pueblo country to a limited extent but with high density along the Rio Grande; the lower Gila Valley, where Pimas practiced irrigated agriculture; the lower Colorado Valley, where Yuman-speaking people used flood-water irrigation; western Washington and Oregon, where fishing provided abundant subsistence; and, surprisingly, large parts of California, despite the absence of either farming or abundant fish. It is clear that the demographic characteristics of all but a few Indians were greatly disrupted by the changes beginning in the late 1700s.

During the 1600s, when intensive contacts with whites began, three centers of higher, more complex culture were flourishing. Contrary to popular belief, the majority of Indians were not wandering nomadic hunters but rather farmers and fishermen, living either in permanent, stable villages or, as among many groups of the eastern woodlands, in stable communities but with frequent moves as they shifted the location of their fields. One center that reached the highest levels of development with respect to religious life, local government, and artistic expression was that of the Pueblo Indians along the Rio Grande and the Little Colorado Rivers (see Fig. 2). Their cultural growth, which was based on the use of irrigated agriculture, can be traced archaeologically in the same region to the early centuries of the Christian era. By the time of the coming of the Spaniards, who found the Pueblos living in large communities of contiguous, masonry buildings of three or four stories, their culture had reached a

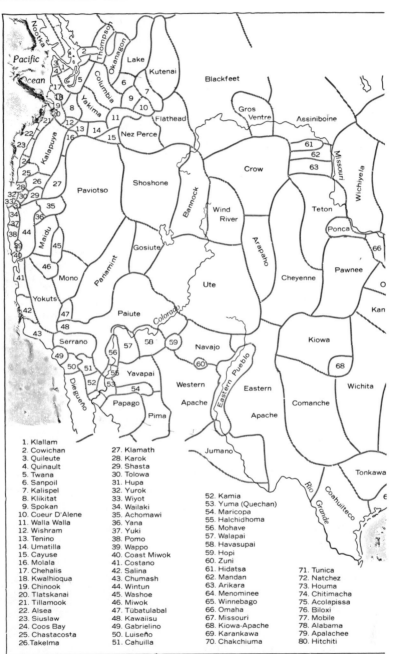

1. Klallam
2. Cowichan
3. Quileute
4. Quinault
5. Twana
6. Sanpoil
7. Kalispel
8. Klikitat
9. Spokan
10. Coeur D'Alene
11. Walla Walla
12. Wishram
13. Tenino
14. Umatilla
15. Cayuse
16. Molala
17. Chehalis
18. Kwalhioqua
19. Chinook
20. Tlatskanai
21. Tillamook
22. Alsea
23. Siuslaw
24. Coos Bay
25. Chastacosta
26. Takelma

27. Klamath
28. Karok
29. Shasta
30. Tolowa
31. Hupa
32. Yurok
33. Wiyot
34. Wailaki
35. Achomawi
36. Yana
37. Yuki
38. Pomo
39. Wappo
40. Coast Miwok
41. Costano
42. Salina
43. Chumash
44. Wintun
45. Washoe
46. Miwok
47. Tübatulabal
48. Kawaiisu
49. Gabrielino
50. Luiseño
51. Cahuilla

52. Kamia
53. Yuma (Quechan)
54. Maricopa
55. Halchidhoma
56. Mohave
57. Walapai
58. Havasupai
59. Hopi
60. Zuni
61. Hidatsa
62. Mandan
63. Arikara
64. Menominee
65. Winnebago
66. Omaha
67. Missouri
68. Kiowa-Apache
69. Karankawa
70. Chakchiuma

71. Tunica
72. Natchez
73. Houma
74. Chitimacha
75. Acolapissa
76. Biloxi
77. Mobile
78. Alabama
79. Apalachee
80. Hitchiti

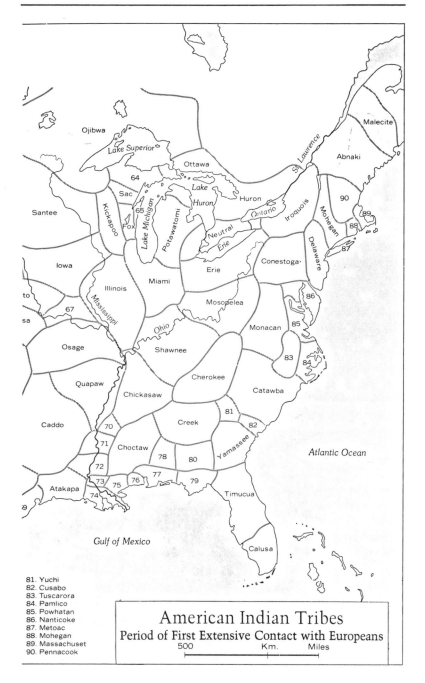

Ojibwa
Malecite
Lake Superior
Ottawa
Abnaki
64
Lake
St. Lawrence
Sac
Huron
90
Santee
Kickapoo
65
Fox
Lake Michigan
Potawatomi
Lake Ontario
Iroquois
Mohegan
89
88
Neutral
Erie
Delaware
87
Iowa
Miami
Erie
Conestoga
86
Illinois
Mosopelea
to
Mississippi
67
Ohio
Monacan
85
sa
Osage
Shawnee
83
84
Quapaw
Cherokee
Catawba
Chickasaw
Caddo
70
Creek
81
82
71
Choctaw
72
78
80
Yamassee
Atakapa
73
75
76
77
79
74
Timucua
9
Gulf of Mexico
Calusa
Atlantic Ocean
Monacan

81. Yuchi
82. Cusabo
83. Tuscarora
84. Pamlico
85. Powhatan
86. Nanticoke
87. Metoac
88. Mohegan
89. Massachuset
90. Pennacook

American Indian Tribes
Period of First Extensive Contact with Europeans

500   Km.   Miles

high point. Even more developed irrigation systems characterized the Piman-speaking peoples in what became southern Arizona. There the agricultural developments and large
communities can be traced back to the 3rd century B.C.

A second center of high cultural growth before the coming
of the whites was in the southeastern United States from the
lower Mississippi Valley east to the Atlantic coast. Here the
Natchez, Choctaw, Creek, and similar peoples were prominent, the Cherokees sharing in the cultural growth somewhat later. The basis of the high culture was again effective
agricultural practices and distinctive forms of political and
social organization. The Creeks' town government lent itself
to political expansion, and with the impetus of European
contacts they became the dominant people of the region.
They had a basically democratic form of political organization that proved capable of absorbing numerous other
peoples. In contrast to the Pueblos, the Creeks, and later the
Choctaws and Cherokees, demonstrated a great capacity for
creative borrowing, not only in their ready utilization of
tools and means of economic production, but also in political
organization. Fusing their own democratic ways with the
formal structure of American democracy, they, along with
others of the region, had by the 1830s evolved culturally to
the point that whites called them the Five Civilized Tribes.
Yet ironically, it was they—the Creeks, Choctaws, Cherokees, Chickasaws, and Seminoles—who were first singled
out for removal to Indian Territory, because their lands,
which included the goldfields of northern Georgia, were the
most coveted by whites.

The third center of important cultural development was
among the Iroquois in what became New York State. About
the time that the French made first contact with Iroquoian-
speaking peoples in the 1500s, and possibly before that, the
Iroquois had initiated a remarkable political confederacy,
and although it was founded on hereditary privilege, the
form that the League of the Iroquois took was highly democratic. Politically united in the league, the five nations of the

Iroquois became an aggressive military power, exerting dominance throughout the Great Lakes region as far as Illinois; for more than a century the Iroquois were a force that all the European nations and the strongest eastern Indians had to reckon with. However, under the stresses of French, British, and American military and cultural pressures, by the end of the American Revolution the league was in a shambles.

The origins of these and other cultural developments are lost in the 10,000 or more years without written record that preceded European contact. The archaeological record gives only the main outline of cultural growth but does not tell us much about the predecessors of the Iroquois and Creeks and their political, religious, and social institutions. Even the continuous record of material growth from 300 B.C. that archaeologists have uncovered in the Southwest does not go far in supplying the details we normally expect in the histories of nations.

According to a widely accepted theory, the Indians of North America reached the continent via the Bering Strait between 10,000 and 20,000 years ago. There is much to support this view, although recent findings, such as the possibility of sailing across the Pacific and the northern Atlantic, suggest greater complexity in the migrations that gave rise to the North American Indian population. However, these theories leave an immense gap in the record—that is, the period between the earliest arrivals and the coming of the Europeans. Very little of importance is known about the cultural origins of the League of the Iroquois before the 16th century or about the Creek and Natchez towns or even about the high cultures of the Southwest earlier than the Christian era. None of the theories provides a historical account comparable to what is known about the origins of the European nations.

However, something is known about important migrations that began about the time of the arrival of the Europeans. From the region of the Great Lakes and the northern

Mississippi Valley, groups of Siouan-speaking peoples were moving westward onto the Great Plains. This movement was accelerated greatly by Chippewas who in response to the French demand for furs pushed from the East for additional hunting grounds. Those who had moved onto the plains found that they could subsist almost wholly on buffalo meat by using the European horse to hunt the vast herds. As horses, guns, and metal knives came into wide use among the new arrivals in the northern plains, a whole new way of life developed rapidly. It was not a diffusion of a European mode of living, but a new Indian creation. The most influential of all American stereotypes of the Indian grew out of this: the feathered headdress, the scalp-collecting warrior, the fabled horsemen of the Plains tribes came to symbolize that nonexistent being, "the American Indian."

The stereotype was broadened somewhat as a result of the settlers' experience with Apaches in the Southwest. A century or more before the Spaniards made their way from Mexico into the Pueblo country, the ancestors of the Apaches of Arizona and New Mexico, who spoke Athapaskan languages, migrated south from Canada. They developed raiding as a way of life and preyed on the Spaniards' villages in New Mexico and farther south. Among the last of the western Indians to be conquered by the U.S. Cavalry, the Apaches, like the Plains Indians, left a tremendous impression on the American imagination, embodied in the thousands of pages written about Cochise and Geronimo. Until they were dominated by whites, Indians like the Apaches and the Sioux were making dynamic adaptations.

The diversity in ways of life before the Europeans arrived was very great, ranging from simple bands of food-gatherers to farmers living in city-states (as the Pueblos have been characterized) and highly organized political confederacies. The diversity is no longer so extreme; common ways of making a living have been adopted, the American legal and political systems have been accepted, and the English language learned by nearly all Indians. Diversity has not, however, disappeared, as the maintenance of 173 different identities indicates.

Aside from distinct histories and experiences, one of the elements of this identification is the continued use of native languages in addition to English. Perhaps half the persisting groups still use the Indian language in the home to some degree, and many others use selected words of an Indian language when referring to things that are part of their cultural heritage. Some languages of each of the 14 major Indian linguistic families are still spoken: Hopi, Pima, Paiute, and others of the far-flung Uto-Aztecan family; Seneca, Cherokee, Onondaga, Tuscarora, and others of the Iroquoian family; Mohave, Quechan, Hualapai, and others of Yuman; Choctaw, Creek, and others of Muskogean—to mention only a few. These major families are as distinct from one another as are the great language families of Europe and Asia. Moreover, the languages of a family such as the Algonkian— Delaware (Lenni Lenape), Narragansett, and Chickahominy —or the Uto-Aztecan—Hopi, Pima, and Yaqui—are mutually unintelligible. Some of this great diversity of language has been lost, as slightly less than one-half of the Indian languages have become extinct, and more are certainly on the way out.

However, a majority of Indians continue to speak an Indian language as well as English. In view of the widespread, violent dislocations of Indian groups and the determined efforts of the Bureau of Indian Affairs (BIA) to root out the Indian languages through formal schooling, it is surprising that so many are still vigorously in use. There are new influences that tend to keep the language diversity alive, among them the development of practical ways of writing. Seven orthographies are in use, for Cherokee, Cree, Creek, Crow, Navajo, Ojibwa, and Lakota (Teton), and others are in process. Interest in writing their languages is high among, for example, Papago, White Mountain Apache, and a dozen others. Indian languages are being taught in the state universities of Arizona, Minnesota, and New Mexico; Northern

Arizona University; Navajo Community College; Pima Community College; and others.

Far more than in language, Indians remain as varied in religious belief and practice as they were when Europeans arrived. Due to the unremitting efforts of missionaries to replace the native religions with Christian denominations, the great majority of Indians profess Roman Catholicism or one of the varieties of Protestantism. But many who profess some form of Christianity also participate in one of the dozen or more native Indian religions that have grown up during the centuries of contact.

The Handsome Lake (or Longhouse) religion among the Iroquois, which came into existence in 1800, is particularly notable, having developed texts in the Seneca language and thousands of adherents among the Six Nations of New York and Canada. More widespread among Indians of different tribes is the Native American church, which in the late 19th century diffused from Mexican Indians among the Kiowas, Delawares, and others in Indian Territory. It has spread to many Oklahoma, Plains, and Midwest groups and more recently to the Navajos, and it maintains a national organization. A central ritual makes use of the hallucinogenic fruit of the peyote cactus and combines Christian with native American belief and ritual. Other religions that have developed during the past century include the Indian Shaker religion of the Northwest; the Drum Dance cult (using sacred songs and dances selected from traditional religions), common in the Midwest among Menominees, Potawatomis, and others; the Silas John cult of the Southwest, which uses giant ground paintings; a variety of modified Medicine Bundle religions, revolving around sacred fetishes owned by clans; and the sacred fire ceremonialism associated with the Keetoowah beliefs of eastern Oklahoma.

Some native religions have maintained with only minor changes their traditional orientations, concepts, and rituals, such as those of the Hopis of Arizona, the Rio Grande Pueblos, the Navajos, the Potawatomis, and the Sioux. Indians in many communities across the country, and particularly in the Southwest, participate only in their native American religions, consciously rejecting Christian beliefs and judging them unfavorably in relation to the Indian ways.

The long-standing diversity in ways of life manifests itself in other respects as well—in preferred house types, such as the Navajo hogan, the Kickapoo wigwam, the Sioux tipi, the Pima sandwich house (walls of earth packed between sticks of desert shrubs), and others; in the use of distinctive dress and footwear; in modes of fishing; in dance and song; and in family values.

Nevertheless, adoption of white ways has been the dominant process over the centuries. At first, borrowing of traits took place through trade and simple proximity. Then the active programs of missionaries, followed by dependence on whites resulting from the destruction of traditional ways of making a living (such as the Plains tribes suffered when the buffalo became extinct) and the imposition of BIA programs to replace Indian ways fostered the loss of Indian and the adoption of white ways. From the 1880s into the 20th century the government programs of forced assimilation were the strongest influence.

It must be emphasized that while forced cultural assimilation brought about replacement of a wide range of Indian ways, it also resulted in extensive alienation of Indians from whites. As Indians borrowed white modes of behavior, belief, and organization, they did not necessarily come to admire whites or identify with them. Rather they identified themselves more intensely as Indians and developed symbols of their identity in the form of religious beliefs, music, dance, selected items of dress like headbands and moccasins, particular ceremonies, and their own heroes and heroines, many of whom were admired because they fought for Indian independence. Each tribe emphasizes symbols associated with events in their historical experience. This vital process has counterbalanced the extensive replacement of cultural elements in Indian life and blocked their absorption by the dominant society.

A question of some importance to Indians is what their

group entities should be called. During the century or two of early European contact, the term nation was in general use for those Indian groups that were land-controlling entities and that had enough internal cohesion to oppose whites or make treaties with them. A nation was made up of Indians who spoke a common language or a set of mutually intelligible dialects and maintained a common set of customs. Such units were regarded by whites as similar to those that were recognized in Europe as nations. However, during the early 19th century Americans began to speak of Indians as "tribes," and this term eventually replaced nation. It had some connotation of inferiority, or in Rudyard Kipling's phrase, a "lesser breed without the Law," and as Indians sensed that, especially by the middle of the 20th century, they rejected the term, and many began to speak again of their groups as nations. The official title of the Navajos and of numerous other Indian entities is now nation, even though the Bureau of Indian Affairs continues to use the term tribe and has officially designated the political bodies it has encouraged as tribal councils. Usage is therefore not consistent and involves political considerations.

To avoid the confusion involved in a general application of either the U.S. government usage or the self-conscious Indian usage, a neutral term such as "ethnic group" is the most useful. By ethnic group is meant a number of people who share a particular Indian group name and other symbols of a common historical experience unique to those who use the group name. Such an identity unit often makes use of a common Indian language and customs and beliefs of Indian origin. However, because of assimilation processes, it may be that the language is replaced and only the historical experience, as symbolized, and the group name remain of the Indian heritage. Nevertheless, the sense of identity among members of culturally assimilated groups may be very intense as a result of alienation from whites. The ethnic group in this sense is of very great importance in understanding developments in Indian–white relations during the 20th century. The 173 entities mentioned at the beginning of this book are considered ethnic groups of this kind.

Eighty years ago the great majority of Indians lived on government reservations, that is, on land owned collectively by Indians but held in trust for them by the Secretary of the Interior. A small minority of Indians lived on state reservations, chiefly in the eastern United States, and others, as in North Carolina, Michigan, Montana, and California, lived in communities that had no special relationship to state or national government. In Oklahoma, where federal reservations were abolished at the end of the 19th century, federal Indian agencies nevertheless were maintained to take care of various land, business, and other interests of Indians. Nowhere was their mobility restricted; Indians were not required by law to live on any of the several kinds of reservations that had been established for them. While there were small towns around agencies on the reservations, and a few Indians had adapted to city life, until World War II nearly all lived under essentially rural conditions on the reservations or in off-reservation communities.

With the possible exception of some of the northern Athapaskan ones in Alaska, all the Indian communities were composed of genetically mixed peoples. Intermixture with Europeans, blacks, and other Indians had been taking place since colonial times and continued in the 20th century. Among some groups, such as the Nanticokes, Chickahominies, Rappahannocks, Mattaponis, Amherst County, Haliwas, Persons County, Houmas, and Seminoles, intermixture with blacks was especially important. Among Pueblos and Indians of southern California, a major genetic element was Mexican, and in other regions the various European strains predominated. By the 1970s, as Indians moved in large numbers to the cities, a new intensified phase of genetic blending had begun.

Even during the rural phase, Indians began to move into the general occupational structure of the United States. On the reservations, opportunities were limited; most Indians on the western reservations were farmers, stock raisers, laborers, or clerical workers in government jobs. In Oklahoma, as the reservations were abolished, Indians began to enter the whole range of American occupations, from business executives, university professors, politicians, and lawyers to the lower-paid white- and blue-collar positions. Only a very few distinctive Indian occupations developed, such as basket- and pottery-making, blanket-weaving, and high-steel construction work.

Movement into American occupations depended heavily on formal schooling. Until the 1930s relatively few Indians were educated for occupations outside the reservations. Indian schools were developed first by the various Christian missions, which reached only a small percentage of Indians during the 19th century. The mission schools were supplemented by schools organized by the Five Civilized Tribes as soon as they became settled in Indian Territory. Until the local tribal governments were abolished by the U.S. government, these were the most advanced school systems west of the Mississippi, and they succeeded in laying a foundation of literacy and elementary education.

The Bureau of Indian Affairs, which assumed responsibility toward the end of the 19th century, relied heavily on boarding schools off the reservations to spearhead the cultural assimilation program. The boarding schools did bring many more Indians into close contact with off-reservation life, but in general they succeeded in orienting only a very few Indians toward the wide range of American occupations. During the 1930s the bureau concentrated on schools on the reservations and also on paying the tuition of Indian children in nearby public schools. These efforts established more and more effective foundations for formal schooling comparable to that of non-Indians. Some tribal councils, such as the Navajo, which began to derive income from oil and gas leasing, provided scholarship funds beginning in the 1940s and 1950s. These, supplemented by BIA scholarship funds, opened up new opportunities in higher education. In 1970 there were 14,191 young Indians in institutions of higher learning, an increase of nearly 300 percent over 1960. Two Indian junior colleges, established during the 1960s among the Navajos and the Sioux, indicated a trend toward placing Indian and non-Indian education on an equal basis.

The next sections are devoted to the Indian ethnic groups as they exist in the 1970s in 12 regions of the United States. In each region the historical experience and cultural background of the groups have distinctive common elements. A few groups have been selected as illustrative of the range of historical experience and current conditions and have been presented in some detail. The selection is not based on any conception of more or less important groups, but rather on the basis of representativeness. In addition, all of the Indian groups living in each region are listed.

PEOPLES OF THE ATLANTIC COAST

In the early 1600s at least 75,000 American Indians lived along the coast from Maine to North Carolina. Divided into approximately 40 groups, they differed from one another in language, customs, and sense of collective identity. However, all of their languages belonged to one linguistic family —Algonkian—and they shared many basic cultural traits, such as the small-scale cultivation of corn, beans, and squash; a religious belief centered on the acquisition of supernatural power through shamans; and a strong tradition of absolutist and hereditary political authority with tribute payments to a principal headman.

In 1970 there were 16 distinct Indian groups in the same area along the Atlantic coast, with a total population of under 10,000. Only two or three of the languages were still in use, although many Algonkian words, such as *pow-wow*, *wigwam, wampum,* and *quahog,* have entered the English language. In general, their cultural characteristics do not readily distinguish them from the surrounding American culture, but each group has a sense of distinctive identity, which in fact has intensified during the past 50 years. Less than 10 percent of the Indian population live on state reservations and none on federal reservations. The great majority live in communities without a special relationship to the government, and many are scattered among the general population.

In New England, there are Indian communities in Maine, Massachusetts, Connecticut, and Rhode Island. Most populous and prominent are the Wampanoag-Mashpees of Massachusetts, the Narragansetts of Rhode Island, and the Penobscots and Passamaquoddies of Maine, in addition to a small cluster of Pequots and Mohegans in Connecticut.

Wampanoag-Mashpees

In 1960 about 1,200 persons in Massachusetts identified themselves as Wampanoags or Wampanoag-Mashpees. They lived in eight communities in the southeastern part of the state—near Mashpee on Cape Cod; at Gay Head and Christian Town on Martha's Vineyard; near Plymouth, Fall River, Dartmouth, New Bedford, and south of Middleboro, all places where Indians had lived at the time of the first English settlement. Claiming descent from some of the reported 20 groups of Algonkian speakers who formed the Wampanoag-dominated federation of tribes during the 1600s, they are genetically much mixed also with whites and blacks. They all speak English, except for the use of Algonkian in ceremonial songs. Their formerly characteristic bark and pole houses, called wigwams, have not been used since the early 1700s. Their clothing, occupations, religious affiliations, and other customs are also not dissimilar from those of the other people in the area.

Their persisting sense of common identity rests in part on

two kinds of distinctive organization. First, Wampanoag tribal councils exist in several communities, such as Mashpee and Gay Head. These representative elected bodies, formally organized in 1972 or earlier from a base of informal leadership groups, are revivals of organizations that existed during the 1940s, the 1860s, and earlier. During the 1970s the Mashpee tribe and the Wampanoag Tribal Council of Gay Head, with the assistance of the Native American Rights Fund, brought suit against the towns of Mashpee and Gay Head for the restoration of land that they claimed had been taken from them illegally. The Wampanoag tribal councils also send delegates to meetings of an organization called the Coalition of Eastern Native Americans.

In addition to this distinctive political organization, the Wampanoag-Mashpees since the 1920s have held an annual pow-wow focusing on intertribal dances, music, and ritual and providing a point of contact with other Indian groups, especially those from the Great Lakes and plains regions. This event has grown in scope and participation, especially during the 1960s. Since 1940 the pow-wow organizers have fostered pageants that portray scenes from Wampanoag history, such as the last stands of Moshup, the Gay Head sachem, and Pometacom (King Philip, d. 1676), leader of the Wampanoag federation and son of Massasoit (d. 1661), who was the first Wampanoag sachem to receive the English, in 1621.

For the modern Wampanoags, Pometacom symbolizes what is most important in their history. Although the period between the arrival of the Pilgrims in 1621 and Massasoit's death was for the most part peaceful under Massasoit's policy of friendly cooperation, the Indians suffered progressive land losses and encroachment, aggressive evangelism, and gradual political subordination. By 1675 Pometacom had quietly organized all the Indians of southeastern Massachusetts for active resistance, and in a bitter two-year war (King Philip's War) most of the Wampanoag leaders were killed, including Pometacom, whose head was cut off and his body quartered (the parts were exhibited at Plymouth for 24 years). Not only was Wampanoag leadership broken, but Indian community life was destroyed, as the English took over the land. King Philip's greatness has become a legend for both parties to the struggle.

Another series of historical events has gained new significance in today's Wampanoag communities. In 1870 Massachusetts passed legislation that resulted in the loss of the land remaining to the Wampanoag-Mashpees; the last community of Indians at Troy, near Fall River, was dispossessed in 1907. A state senate investigation begun in 1861 decided that the Indians had become self-sufficient economically, having adopted the occupations of surrounding peoples. It also found that there had been much intermixture with blacks and others, although the Indians had tried unsuccessfully to prohibit intermixture. On this basis, sentiment developed in the legislature for abolishing the reservations established by the state in the 1700s and eliminating state aid for schooling and welfare. Despite the fact that the Indian majority voted against the breakup of the reservations (their consent was required by previous agreement), the legislature proceeded to dissolve them. In 1976 these state actions came under legal review with the filing of the suits by the Mashpee and Gay Head councils. A jury decision in 1977 went against the Indians on the grounds that they were not a tribe, but the case was appealed and awaits final decision.

Narragansetts

The Narragansetts in 1970 numbered approximately 400 persons who lived for the most part in a community at Charlestown, R.I. Every August there is a pow-wow in Charlestown, where ceremonial dances are an important activity. The present-day dances, music, and costumes, like those of the Wampanoags, bear little resemblance to 17th-century practice; they are strongly influenced by plains and other western Indians, as well as by Iroquois. Before the 1970s periodic efforts were made to revive Narragansett ceremonialism.

The Narragansetts maintain a community house, called a longhouse, where tribal meetings and annual elections of councilmen are held. The council deals with internal affairs and relations with other Indian tribes concerning the annual pow-wow, and for two years it published a newspaper called *The Narragansett Dawn*. The group maintains a Methodist church with a Narragansett minister and a committee that manages church affairs. In 1926 the Narragansetts organized a local chapter of the Algonquin Council of Indian Tribes, which gave impetus to the pow-wows, held on the church grounds, and turned them toward an intertribal emphasis.

The Indian Reorganization Act of 1934 (IRA) stimulated tribal organization, although because the Narragansetts do not live on federal trust land, they were not required to have a tribal council. Their church and community organizations provide a channel of communication and a means for maintaining their strong sense of Narragansett identity, which has been sustained for 370 years.

The Narragansetts are completely assimilated culturally in housing, dress, and almost all other aspects of culture. They have not spoken the Narragansett language for at least a hundred years and do not, in contrast with the Wampanoags, have ceremonial songs that preserve the language. They are much mixed genetically with whites, blacks, and some other Indians and have absorbed several other Indian groups, most notably the Niantics.

The Narragansetts were rivals of the Wampanoags and kept themselves distinct, but they joined them in the 1675 war against the English, who had executed their most respected leader, Miantonomo, in 1643. Because of this longstanding grievance and a growing sense of helplessness in the face of English encroachments, the Narragansetts welcomed King Philip's War. They maintained their own separate command but joined actively in support of the Wampanoags; as a result they were nearly exterminated even

before Pometacom was defeated. After the war the Narragansetts became increasingly subject to supervision by the
English, as their few remaining younger sagamores, or hereditary chiefs, sold one piece of land after another.

By 1709 they held only one very small parcel, which was
made into a reservation, where their population very slowly
increased over the next century. The Indians built a Methodist church there and maintained a community government.
In 1776, the hereditary chiefs having grown irresponsible,
the system of sagamore leadership was changed to the
elected representative council form (as it remains today).
From 1792 the state regulated the election of council members and arranged for a commissioner to represent Narragansett interests before the state legislature.

In 1879 the community voted to abolish its tribal status.
Two years later the state confirmed their action and proceeded to break into individual allotments the 1,000 acres
that had been held jointly since colonial times. Thus the
state reservation was eliminated, but the community organization continued, adopting the designation Narragansett
Tribe. It was this organization that brought suit in 1976 for
recovery of Narragansett lands on the grounds that the state
of Rhode Island had acted illegally in breaking up the reservation and dispossessing the Indians of other lands as well.
In 1978 the case was settled out of court with the award of
1,900 acres to the Narragansetts in trust.

Penobscots

In Maine there are two state reservations inhabited by
peoples who preceded whites into the area. In addition there
are more than a thousand Malecite and Micmac Indians,
who over many years have migrated from Canada. They
have no reservations and no special relationship with the
U.S. government. In 1970 the Penobscots numbered between 600 and 700, living chiefly in one major community on
a reservation near Old Town on the Penobscot River, an area

where they have concentrated since 1669. The state-supervised, 4,481-acre reservation is a portion of the land in which they formerly lived and hunted.

Within the community the Penobscots maintain a political system of their own devising and speak of themselves as the Penobscot Nation. The government consists of the Old Party and the New Party, which take turns every two years controlling the community government. The party in power, served by a single council house, elects a governor, a council, and a representative to the Maine state legislature. In 1975 the Penobscot Nation sued the state for recovery of some 10 million acres that it claimed had been taken from them without the approval of the U.S. Congress, as required by the Indian Nonintercourse Act of 1790. During 1978 the Penobscot attorneys, the state of Maine, and representatives of the federal government negotiated a settlement.

The Penobscots are for the most part bilingual, speaking an Indian language and English. A few families speak Penobscot, but most use Malecite, the language of Indians of northern Maine and Canada who have intermarried extensively with Penobscots. In contrast with Massachusetts Indians, a high proportion of Penobscots are of purely Indian descent, chiefly Penobscot-Malecite or Penobscot-Passamaquoddy mixtures. Most Penobscot cultural traits have been replaced, but much hunting, fishing, forest, and sea lore has been retained and is vital to the important occupation of guiding people through the Maine woods. Another major source of employment is a woolen mill that was built near the Penobscot settlements in 1889.

During colonial times the Penobscots were the largest group of northern Algonkian speakers in their region. They were active in a confederation of Indian nations formed to combat Iroquois expansion; this confederation, however, was dominated by Abnakis and bore their name, despite the numerical importance of Penobscots. They were involved with the French and other Indians against the English, who in the 1740s offered bounties for Penobscot scalps. In 1749, however, a general peace was made between the English and the Penobscots. After the French and Indian War in the late 1700s, when most tribes of western Maine migrated to Canada, land cessions reduced their former large territory to disconnected bits, including islands in the Penobscot River and the community near Old Town. From a reported 1,000 individuals in 1736, the Penobscot population declined to 387 by 1900. Their numbers had almost doubled by 1970.

Passamaquoddies

In 1970 approximately 700 Passamaquoddies lived in two communities on a state reservation in southeastern Maine near Passamaquoddy Bay. Each community has a local governing body: the Indian Township Tribal Council and the Pleasant Point Tribal Council; in addition there are a Passamaquoddy tribal council and a governor elected by popular vote. While the Passamaquoddy language is spoken by some families, all of these Indians speak English, and many speak Malecite and Micmac. They participate regularly in powwows of other eastern Indian groups. They are culturally assimilated to the ways of neighboring whites to about the same degree as the Penobscots.

The Passamaquoddies were not involved in much warfare during the colonial period, although some fought in the Revolution on the side of the Americans. A treaty with the United States in 1777 included a guarantee of their lands in perpetuity, but this treaty was never ratified by Congress. Beginning in 1794, individual chiefs began signing agreements with Maine and Massachusetts to cede all of their extensive hunting territory for no compensation whatever. Ultimately the Indians controlled only an 18,000-acre tract, which, when the state of Maine was formed, was recognized as a state reservation. In 1971, working with the Native American Rights Fund, the Passamaquoddy Tribe initiated a suit against the state for recovery of the land that had been signed away without the approval of Congress. In 1975 the

U.S. Department of Justice supported the suit and arranged to give assistance in prosecution or negotiation. The case influenced other Indian groups of the eastern United States to bring suits on a similar basis. In 1978 a compromise on the land claim was reached with the state.

Nanticokes

During the 18th and early 19th centuries the Indians of the Middle Atlantic states—the Mahicans, the large Lenni Lenape (Delaware) Nation, and the Conestoga, for example— were almost entirely eliminated. By the 1970s only three small groups remained in these states—the Poosepatuck and Shinnecock, numbering less than 150 each on tiny state reservations on Long Island, N.Y., and the Nanticokes of southern Delaware.

The Nanticokes in the 1970s numbered between 400 and 500. They live along the Indian River in an area they had occupied at the coming of the Europeans. Their land is individually owned, and they have worked for many years in the local occupations, chiefly farming, chicken raising, and various kinds of wage work. The Nanticokes, who no longer speak the Nanticoke language, have intermarried with both whites and blacks. Some native customs survive, especially among those engaged in fishing, chiefly the customary law regarding use rights along the rivers and a belief in dreams as a mode of establishing relations with the wildlife of the area. Other traditions, such as matrilineal descent of social status and property, have entirely disappeared. All of the Nanticokes are nominal Christians. Generally classed by local whites as colored and on that basis excluded from white schools until the 1950s, some Nanticokes formed the Nanticoke Indian Association, which was successful in eliminating segregation. However, a segment of the community preferred to identify with blacks, and a division along those lines continues to exist in the community.

The Nanticokes were one of the Algonkian-speaking

coastal groups of the Chesapeake Bay that were strongly hostile to the early white settlers. Their hostilities culminated in war in 1742 when they, along with the Choptanks and the Conoys, were defeated, and Maryland established a reservation for them. The Nanticokes split into three bands; one group joined the Delawares and went with them during their westward migrations to Texas and Indian Territory. Another group, associated primarily with the Conoys, moved north, establishing temporary settlements (sometimes still known as "Nanticoke Towns") in Pennsylvania and New York. By 1781 this band was at Fort Niagara, N.Y., where they lived under the protection of the Iroquois. Shortly after, they moved into Canada and were merged among the Iroquois in the Six Nations Reserve. The third group returned from the Maryland reservation to their traditional territory in southern Delaware and settled as fishermen and tenant farmers. After 1865, when the plantations were broken up, they bought land, which they still own. Culturally they have steadily assimilated into the rural life of the area, but they preserve a strong sense of Indian identity in their daily lives.

Chickahominies

Five different, formerly Algonkian-speaking peoples lived in Virginia in the 1970s. In 1960 more than 3,000 persons were recorded as identifying as Indians, but the 1970 census estimated barely 2,000. The great majority live in independent communities outside the two state reservations.

The most numerous of the Virginia Indians in 1970 were the Chickahominies, of whom there were about 500, the same population as in 1923, living southeast of Richmond. The people, much mixed with blacks, whites, and other local Indian groups, made a determined effort in the late 19th century to avoid being categorized as Negro by the state and were successful, with the assistance of their Baptist church connection and the county government, in having themselves classified as Indians. They maintain a tribal organization with elected representatives. During the past 75 to 80 years they have become increasingly culturally assimilated, ceasing to speak their Algonkian language and generally adopting white ways. Only with respect to fishing, hunting, and some farming practices have traditional ways of thought and practice been retained. Since the 1920s they have engaged in pow-wows of eastern Indians and through such activities have revived an interest in native dances, music, and ceremonial costume.

At the time of European settlement, the Chickahominies lived on the southern margin of the settlements controlled by the chief Powhatan (c. 1550–1618). However, they maintained their own separate tribal organization and in the early 1600s were probably the largest Indian nation in Virginia. Renouncing ties with Powhatan in 1613, they made a treaty with the English in which they agreed to be "forever called Englishmen." When a new English governor tried to exact more tribute from them, however, they resisted and became involved in hostilities between the English and Powhatan's people, under the leadership of Opechancanough of the Pamunkeys. The major settlement of the Chickahominies was destroyed by the British, Openchancanough was disastrously defeated, and the Pamunkeys made a treaty ceding all the lands of the Powhatan Confederacy to the English. The Chickahominies withdrew from further contact, but settlers moving into the interior overwhelmed them, and by 1660 they were almost landless. The English gave them a grant of land not in their traditional territory, but to the north in former Pamunkey territory, and placed them under the domination of the Pamunkeys. Their independent position deteriorated thereafter; by 1750 they had lost their reservation, their several towns had been reduced to one, and their population was apparently less than 300. By the end of the 1700s it seemed that the Chickahominy language, style of dress, and other ways were lost. They were landless, poverty-stricken wanderers, and yet through all their troubles they retained a tribal organization. Around 1800 all the remaining Chickahominies were converted by a Baptist evangelist, whose activities were stimulated by the second Great Awakening, which was then sweeping the American frontier.

During the last half of the 19th century the Chickahominies drifted back to their traditional territory and formed two communities, each with a Baptist church as the center of community life. Their traditional organization had disintegrated, but they organized themselves sufficiently to adopt measures that emphasized their Indian identity, such as wearing their hair long and barring intermarriage and social mingling with blacks. During the 1880s they began to revive the use of Indian given names. By the end of the 19th century the state of Virginia began to make certain distinctions in law between Indians and blacks, and a separate Indian school was established for them.

In the early 20th century, anthropologists James Mooney and Frank Speck encouraged them to reinstitute their traditional form of tribal organization. Further impetus in this direction came from the Algonquin Council of Indian Tribes, which was first organized in the 1920s by their neighbors, the Rappahannocks.

Pamunkeys

In any description of their history and present condition, the Pamunkeys cannot be readily separated from their immediate neighbors, the Rappahannocks and the Mattaponis. In 1970 these three groups numbered approximately 2,000 to 3,000. Fewer than a hundred each of Pamunkeys and Mattaponis live on the two state reservations established for them. The others are scattered through tidewater Virginia between Richmond and the coast from the James River to the Rappahannock. Five distinct communities exist, organized as tribes and affiliated with Baptist churches. The reservation-dwelling Pamunkeys and Mattaponis each speak of themselves as a tribe and maintain organizations that in some features resemble the organization that existed in the 1600s when the Pamunkeys were politically dominant. Most of the reservation dwellers, who are accorded higher status than the scattered families, are farmers, and some are in small business; all engage in fishing. Their housing and other traits are like those of the surrounding American culture. English is the only language used.

The Pamunkeys were the heirs of the Powhatan Confederacy, which was reported by the early English settlers as consisting of some 30 nations whose population was estimated as high as 9,000 to 10,000. These nations were probably small groups of villages with local names that distinguished one group from another; they may have spoken different dialects. Powhatan, a hereditary leader, headed the confederacy at the time of the founding of Jamestown in 1607. He was regarded by the English as a king, and his family constituted a royal line. His relations with the English, at first hostile, improved after his niece, Pocahontas (1595?–1617), married John Rolfe. But an undercurrent of hostility was continually fed by small clashes between Indians and outposts of English settlers, usually over land encroachments. When Opechancanough succeeded Powhatan in 1618, the clashes intensified, and in 1622 Opechancanough unsuccessfully led some Pamunkeys in organized resistance. For the next 20 years the English regularly destroyed Indian crops and laid waste their fields. Both sides were guilty of frequent killings.

In 1644, when the last Indian resistance was contained and Opechancanough was killed, the confederacy completely disintegrated, and the English introduced direct rule over them. The Indians still thought in terms of a Pamunkey royal line, with hegemony over all the Indians of Virginia, even though the English were wholly dominant. The Pamunkeys' status as the leading nation was emphasized by their successful defeats of the Iroquois, who raided Virginia in the late 17th century. In peace treaties signed by the British, the Iroquois, and other Indians in 1685 and 1722, the Pamunkeys were officially accorded this special status.

The English made vigorous efforts to culturally assimilate the Pamunkeys and associated Virginia peoples during the 18th century. In 1714 the Pamunkeys agreed to send 20 young men every year to study at William and Mary College. The Pamunkeys and others formally agreed to become Christians, and active proselytizing by various Protestant denominations continued through the century. By 1727 an official interpreter was regarded as no longer necessary in the courts and elsewhere, and the office was abolished, not because the Algonkian languages had disappeared, but because many Indians had become bilingual. The village groups had been displaced from their territories and were no longer in touch with one another. By the end of the century many Virginians believed that the Pamunkeys would disappear in a few years.

They did not disappear, however. Although the Pamunkeys and other Indians worked in many of the occupations common in the tidewater area, such as sailing, fishing, and various kinds of skilled work, the Pamunkeys and Rappahannocks especially continued to maintain a distinct Indian identity. This effort was powerfully stimulated by their desire not to be classified and treated as Negroes and, like that of the Chickahominies, it met with some success. They have retained their Indian identity and some degree of continuity in the traditional Algonkian political and community organization. The process has also been aided by the state's creation of reservations for Pamunkeys and Mattaponis, which, although few live on them, provide stable political centers. The Rappahannocks in the 1920s made a wider Indian identification, participating in the formation of the Algonquin Council of Indian Tribes, which brought the Virginia nations together again.

Other Atlantic coast Indians in the 1970s were the following: the Malecites and Micmacs of Maine; the Montauks,

Poosepatucks, and Shinnecocks of New York; the Mattaponis and Rappahannocks of Virginia; the Nipmucs of Massachusetts; and the Paugusetts, Pequots, Mohegans, and
Scaticooks of Connecticut.

THE DEPOPULATED SOUTHEAST

In 1970 in the area extending from the Atlantic coast to the
Mississippi River and, excluding Virginia, from the Ohio
River south to the Gulf of Mexico, there were eight distinct
Indian groups with a total population of less than 40,000.
One of them—the Lumbees—numbered almost 30,000; the
population of the other groups was about 6,500–7,000. This
large region is one of small Indian population, in sharp contrast to the early years of contact with Europeans. During the
17th and 18th centuries it was one of the most heavily populated Indian regions, with as many as 23 distinct Indian
peoples at the time of the beginning of the European invasions. Two-thirds of the groups apparently have been eliminated, and a population estimated at more than 150,000 reduced by more than two-thirds. If, because of their peculiar
circumstances, we set aside the Lumbees for the moment,
the Indian population may be said to have declined by about
90 percent.

This great contrast between conditions in the late 17th and
the mid-20th centuries came about largely because the
southeastern states were the scene in the 19th century of the
most thoroughgoing application of the removal policy.
These states were President Andrew Jackson's home territory, and it was he who set out to clear the region of Indians.
His policy was popular with the whites, because of the tremendous land boom in the 1830s, stimulated by cotton production. Although not totally successful, the policy did remove the region's largest and most "civilized" tribes. By
1970 Kentucky, Tennessee, Georgia, and West Virginia had

no Indian communities; Alabama had only a scattered few, and South Carolina had but one small community. Only three states—North Carolina, Florida, and Mississippi—had numbers comparable to those of the surviving Indian groups in the coastal states of the Northeast.

Eastern Band of Cherokees

In 1960, in the mountainous southwest corner of North Carolina, there were 4,266 Cherokees living on a federal reservation of 44,000 acres. Residents of this reservation constitute a small minority of the former Cherokee nation; the great majority was deported in the 1830s to Indian Territory. The official name of the North Carolina group is Eastern Band of Cherokees.

The Eastern Band was organized in the manner of most Indians on federal reservations who formed tribal councils under the regulations of the IRA in the 1930s. The Eastern Band has a constitution and a tribal council whose primary function is the regulation of land usage. Elected for terms of two years by popular vote of reservation residents, council members represent the six towns into which the reservation is divided. All who can prove one-thirty-second Cherokee descent are eligible to vote. There are also Free Labor Companies, based on the traditional *gadugi*, social units that cooperate with each other in labor exchange. A chief and a vice-chief are elected every four years.

One of the chief's functions is to serve as president of the Fair Association, which sponsors an annual fair designed to encourage the Cherokee farmers in agricultural pursuits and to revive some traditional entertainments, such as the stickball game. A Cherokee Historical Association maintains a museum that presents exhibits on Cherokee history and culture and sponsors a summer production of *Unto These Hills*, a historical drama that attracts millions of tourists every year. Many ceremonial dances have been revived.

Most Cherokees are members of Baptist churches, and

some are Holiness, Methodist, or Episcopal church members, but many also participate in traditional religious dances and ceremonies. Cherokee religion as an integrated whole has disappeared. The Cherokee language is used in the home by perhaps 50 percent of the families, although many of them also speak English. The syllabary devised by the leader Sequoyah (1770?–1843) is used by some individuals, even though an effort to teach it along with the Cherokee language in the schools has failed. Bibles written in the syllabary are used by many older people.

When the main body of Cherokees was forcibly removed from their territory in northern Georgia during 1833–1838, about 1,000 fugitives scattered into North Carolina and were never deported. Many of these were followers of Yonahguski, a conservative peace leader who, yielding to the intense pressures that had built up for Indian land cessions by 1819, had signed a treaty ceding a large amount of land to Georgia. Yonahguski was awarded a personal holding of 640 acres at the important ancient town site of Kituhwa, which became the nucleus of the area in which the fugitives settled.

When Yonahguski died in 1839, a white trader named William Thomas, who had lived among the Cherokees for some 20 years, undertook to legalize the fugitives' residence in North Carolina and to secure more land for them. Five towns of the traditional Cherokee type were established in the vicinity of what became the federal reservation, but there was no formal organization until 1861. In 1870 Cherokee efforts to organize the five towns resulted in a tribal government, which was incorporated in 1889. Meanwhile, the U.S. commissioner of Indian affairs had taken note of the Eastern Band and had become trustee for their lands, which were all secured by individual deeds.

In 1881 the Society of Friends established schools, and a majority of Cherokees became bilingual. Most became small-scale farmers, raising cattle and hogs, but by the 1920s conditions for this kind of farming had deteriorated, and the Cherokee standard of living steadily declined. It was not

until the early 1950s that the tourist business resulted in relative economic prosperity. By this time their houses and general lifestyle closely approximated that of rural whites of the
region.

The reservation is by no means culturally homogeneous,
however. Lifestyles and world views range from that of the
full-bloods, who constitute about one-fourth of the population, to that of what some observers call middle-class Indians. The latter, a very small part of the population, are employed in nonfarming business and in the reservation offices
of the Bureau of Indian Affairs. The majority are oriented to
both sets of values, expressing one or the other extreme in
different circumstances at different times. Some think of
themselves as Indians and attend Indian pow-wows across
the United States, but are not fully at ease with the ways of
the full-bloods. Some identify with Indians at times but are
more fully oriented toward the local rural white way of life.

Lumbees

In 1970 about 31,000 Lumbees lived in southeastern North
Carolina, constituting the principal element in the population of Robeson County, where they live in small towns and
as scattered rural families. The major concentration is in and
around the town of Pembroke. About 600–700 live immediately over the state line in South Carolina, and another 2,000
recent emigrants from Robeson County live in Baltimore.

The Lumbees are a nearly unique group of Indians in the
United States. Although they identify themselves very definitely as Indians, no vestige of an Indian language is spoken
among them, nor is there any conclusive historical or ethno-
logical evidence that they have ever spoken an Indian language. One supposition is that their ancestors spoke a
Siouan language, and another that the ancient language was
Algonkian. The name Lumbee itself is of unknown origin
and has never been attributed to any tribal group on record.
The major river flowing through Robeson County is offi-

cially named the Lumber River, although the Indians call it the Lumbee, leading to speculation that they derived their name from the river. Investigators during the 19th century became convinced that the Lumbees were derived from the "Croatan Indians" of the Cape Hatteras area and persuaded the North Carolina legislature in 1885 to officially name them the "Croatans." The Indians rejected the designation, because there never was such an Indian group. In 1911 the legislature also rejected the name Croatan and officially named them Indians of Robeson County.

The Lumbees maintain that they are of mixed origin, combining an unknown Indian element with that of the lost colony founded in Roanoke Island in 1587 by John White, which was never definitely identified thereafter. The first records that clearly cite the Lumbees are land grants to individuals beginning in 1732. There was no indication that they used any other language than English at that time. Their physical appearance ranges from clearly European to a dark-skinned type classified as Indian, which led to their suffering the same disabilities as Negroes during the 19th century. In the 20th century they have been the victims of discrimination in some places, and the Ku Klux Klan has burned crosses in their communities.

A notable characteristic of the Lumbees has been a strong sense of solidarity. This became especially apparent after 1835, when the North Carolina Constitutional Convention, responding to fears generated by slave insurrections and abolitionist activities, excluded nonwhites from political participation and the benefits of citizenship. For the next 50 years Lumbees were disfranchised and denied schools. Tensions mounted in Robeson County, culminating during the 1860s in what became known as the Lowrie War. The hero of this series of conflicts, from the Lumbee perspective, was Henry Berry Lowrie, who led a band of Lumbees in guerrilla warfare in the county until he mysteriously disappeared in 1872.

It was not until 1885 that the status of Lumbees as Indians

began to receive attention. Funds were made available for the development of a school, first called the Croatan Normal School and later renamed Pembroke State College. As the college improved and became the major educational influence in the area, Lumbees gradually took the important roles in its faculty and administration. In the meantime they regained the right to vote, and in the 1880s they began to organize the Christian religious life that they had carried on, without benefit of churches, for more than a century. In 1880 what became the Burnt Swamp Baptist Association, the major Lumbee church organization, was organized to unite the Baptist communities in Robeson County. By the 1970s there were also Methodist, Assembly of God, Holiness, and other churches. There seems never to have been any form of native Indian religion or ceremony.

In the 1950s some Lumbees began to believe that the group was descended from the Tuscaroras, who had migrated from eastern North Carolina to join the Iroquois Confederacy. They held that some Tuscaroras had stayed behind, moved west, and become the ancestors of the Lumbees. Mad Bear, a well-known militant leader of the New York Tuscaroras, visited the Lumbees in 1954, encouraged them in this belief, and urged more vigorous efforts to establish their status as Indians through federal recognition. The Lumbees of the 1970s, who by then had a relatively high level of formal education, campaigned for recognition by the federal government which, in the late 1970s had not been conferred.

Catawbas

The population of the Catawbas, the only group of Indians in South Carolina, except for scattered Lumbee families, was listed in 1970 as 631, but the tribal roll that year carried 1,334 individuals. Most live on individually owned land near Rock Hill in the northern part of the state, but some live on a 640-acre tract that was once a state reservation and is now collectively owned. Since 1900 no one has spoken the original Siouan language. The Catawbas are almost wholly culturally assimilated, working in industry or engaged in farming, small business, or clerical work. Nearly all are Mormons, having been converted by missionaries in the 1880s. Their political organization consists of the Catawba Nation Executive Tribal Committee and a popularly elected general assembly. Elections are held once a year, but the chairman, vice-chairman, and two councilors serve staggered terms of one, three, and four years. They hold no pow-wow of their own and, except for attendance at the Eastern Cherokee Fall Festival each year, rarely participate in other Indian pow-wows.

During the late 17th century they were reputed to have been a nation of 6,000 and were rated by the English as one of the four great nations of the region. They increased rapidly in numbers and prestige during the early 1700s, and they took into a confederacy and ultimately absorbed a number of Siouan-speaking peoples from the Atlantic coast to the mountains. They supported the English against the Tuscaroras in 1711 but joined with the Creeks and others in the Yamassee War against the English in 1715, which involved all the Indians from North Carolina down the coast to St. Augustine, Fla. The Catawbas extricated themselves before a crushing defeat of the other Indians and thereafter supported the English. Although distinguished fighters, they suffered serious defeats by the Senecas in 1737 and, as smallpox epidemics hit them, lost population heavily. During the next 25 years they declined to barely 400 people, who were dependent on the English and sought their protection in Virginia.

In 1763, at the close of the French and Indian War, they made a treaty with the colony of South Carolina, which assured them of 144,000 carefully bounded acres containing the site of the former capital of their six towns. They maintained a tribal government on this land, and two of their headmen, Young Warrior and "King" Hagler, became well known. Their numbers continued to decline; they leased most of their land to whites and became increasingly dependent on the state. In 1840, after years of pressure for Indian removal, they made a treaty with South Carolina, which provided that the state would pay them $5,000 for their 144,000 acres if they would leave the state. The Catawbas were anxious to join the Five Civilized Tribes in their move to Indian Territory, but the Cherokees rejected them, although a few Catawbas settled among the Eastern Band. The Choctaws accepted a few, who moved west with them. Some very small groups on their own initiative moved to Colorado and Utah, where they still preserve their identity, their number being less than 100. The fewer than 100 who remained in South Carolina were ultimately given a state reservation of 640 acres of very poor land, but no assistance of any kind for nearly 50 years. Throughout their ordeals they maintained the office of chief and an elected council.

In 1941 the Bureau of Indian Affairs took over their jurisdiction. It secured 2,500 acres of better land, over which it assumed trusteeship and introduced a constitution and tribal government but supplied no services. In 1959 the Catawba Tribal Committee asked that tribal assets be divided among the individuals but that federal recognition be maintained. In 1961 the newly acquired land was distributed, and the BIA withdrew from jurisdiction, but the tribe retained ownership of the 640-acre reservation.

In 1904 the Catawba Nation advanced a claim against the state for the 144,000 acres taken as a result of the treaty of 1840. In 1972 this claim was renewed, with the aid of the Native American Rights Fund, in the form of a suit for restoration of the land or compensation. In the late 1970s the suit was still unresolved.

Seminoles and Miccosukees

In 1967 there were 1,350 Indians in Florida, 1,000 identifying as Seminoles and 350 as Miccosukees. Most of the Seminoles live on three federal reservations, one at the western edge of Lake Okeechobee and two near the Big Cypress Swamp in southern Florida. The Miccosukees live on several parcels of land near the Everglades under a single BIA administration. A state reservation exists, but it is not much used. In addition, some 400 Indians live along the Tamiami Trail and elsewhere in independent communities.

Both the Seminoles and Miccosukees are organized under the IRA with constitutions and tribal councils. Their lands are held by tribal titles under federal trust. The Seminoles speak a Muskogean language related to Creek, the Miccosukees a language of the Hitchiti family. Many are nominal members of Southern Baptist congregations, but native religious participation is common, especially in the all-night dance-ground ceremony derived from the Creek religion. Traditional dress and palm thatch houses (called *chikee* by many whites) are common. A return to native crafts has been encouraged since the 1960s, such as basketry, beadwork, leather goods, and patchwork. As an important tourist attraction, exhibition villages in aboriginal style have been established both on and off the reservation. Since 1959 there has been much interest in pan-Indian pow-wows. Although they often live near one another, the Seminoles and Miccosukees maintain separate identities, reinforced by the use of different languages.

Neither the Seminoles nor the Miccosukees are native to the area. At the time of the European invasions, Florida was occupied by tribes that became extinct from disease, enslavement, deportation to the West Indies, and warfare. Beginning in the late 1600s, members of the Creek Confederacy began to raid from the north and then settle in the region that the Spaniards controlled and called Florida. The Creek settlement continued through the 18th century, first in the north around Tallahassee and what is now Gainesville but steadily extending southward into central Florida. Among the Creek-affiliated settlers were some speakers of Hitchiti languages, the ancestors of the Miccosukees. The Musko-

gean-speaking pioneers among the Creeks were the fore-
bears of the reservation-dwelling Seminoles. The term Seminole was not an aboriginal tribal name but came from the
Spanish word *cimarrón*, perhaps with the broad meaning of
frontiersmen or pioneers, as used by the Creeks.

These Indians from the north retained their languages and
way of life with a minimum of European influence until well
into the 19th century. In 1814, after Andrew Jackson's defeat
of the conservative Redstick faction of the Creeks, several
hundred refugees made their way south to join the Florida
Indians. The U.S. government turned its attention in this direction, both because the Americans wished to eliminate the
Spaniards from their southern border and also because the
region had become a haven for escaped slaves. These con-
cerns sparked what was called the First Seminole War in
1817–1818, in which U.S. troops destroyed the Muskogean-
speaking towns from the coast west to Tallahassee. After the
United States acquired Florida in 1819, the federal government made an agreement with the Seminoles. Although the
Indians had no central governing body, the United States
forced them to cede all claims to land in Florida in return for
a reservation in the central swampland. However, the reservation was never established.

According to the government, the situation in Florida had
not improved: the Indians were accused of harboring slaves
and there were some raids, which eventually led to the Second Seminole War in 1835. The war lasted seven years and
was extremely costly to the government because of the very
great difficulties imposed by the terrain. By 1842 U.S. troops
had rounded up 4,420 Indians, along with many blacks, and
deported them to Indian Territory in accord with Jackson's
policy of forced removal, where they became known as one
of the Five Civilized Tribes. Only 500 Indians remained in
the vicinity of the Big Cypress Swamp in extreme southwestern Florida. In 1860 the Third Seminole War resulted in
the deportation of 240 more Indians and blacks, leaving 200–
300 in the most impenetrable region of all—the Everglades.

The Bureau of Indian Affairs in 1891 began to seek land for the remnant of Florida Indians and ultimately established three reservations, but as late as 1930 only 10 percent had accepted bureau supervision. Even in 1970 more than a quarter of the Indians preferred to live off the reservations.

Other Indians of the Southeast in the 1970s were the Altamahas of Georgia, some Creeks of Alabama, and the Choctaws of Mississippi.

THE IROQUOIS OF THE EASTERN GREAT LAKES COUNTRY

On the U.S. side of Lakes Ontario and Erie in the 1970s there were Indians only in the state of New York; the Conestogas, Eries, Neutrals, and other Indians of Pennsylvania and Ohio had disappeared from the region. Those who live in New York are Iroquoian-speaking peoples; numbering at least 10,300, they live on eight state-supervised reservations and in widely scattered families throughout the state and in Brooklyn. They identify broadly as Iroquois (descendants of the League of the Iroquois) but primarily as belonging to one of six distinct tribal groups—Mohawk, Onondaga, Cayuga, Oneida, Seneca, and Tuscarora—as had their ancestors at least since the 1500s. The six groups are officially designated as nations in New York State.

The total Iroquois population in the 1970s was between 20,000 and 25,000. Besides those in New York, somewhat fewer than 10,000 live in Canada, 3,500 in Wisconsin, and 900–1,000 in Oklahoma. Although the history and present life of the Canadian and New York Iroquois are not separable, the following discussion is confined mainly to those in New York. Of the six distinct national or tribal identities, the Mohawks, Onondagas, Tuscaroras, and Senecas have their own reservations; the Cayugas have no reservation, but the 303 listed members of that nation in 1970 lived on one of the Senecas' reservations; the Oneidas have no reservation in New York but do have some tax-exempt land on which 129 individuals live, while 470 others live on the Onondagas' reservation. Another 3,500 Oneidas live in Wisconsin on their own reservation.

Until recently the Senecas were the largest of the six nations, with a population of 4,600 on three reservations in western New York. The Mohawks were the second largest, with an official population of 2,229 on a single reservation along the St. Lawrence River; they call themselves the St. Regis Band of Mohawks. Some 800 Mohawks from the Caughnawaga Reservation in Canada live in Brooklyn. The Onondagas numbered 900 on one reservation, and the Tuscaroras, about 700 on their reservation. The progressive loss of their once-vast hunting territories after early contact with whites has been a major theme of Iroquois life. However, only the Tuscaroras have been completely displaced from their former homeland in eastern North Carolina.

The Iroquoian languages are spoken in some homes in all of the groups, including the Brooklyn community of Mohawks, with the highest proportion of Iroquoian-speakers among the Senecas and the Mohawks. Probably most adult Iroquois are bilingual, and many know two or three Indian languages as well as English.

Their lifestyle has changed profoundly since the time of the fur trade in the 18th century, and there has been a great deal of cultural assimilation. Twentieth-century ranch-style and suburban houses mingle with earlier 19th-century frame farmhouses. Incomes vary widely, as Iroquois have moved into a wide range of occupations as professionals, white-collar workers, and skilled and unskilled labor in various businesses. Their most distinctive specialty is high-steel construction work on bridges and skyscrapers. Iroquois belong to many different Christian churches, the Mohawks being predominantly Catholic. However, more than half of the New York Iroquois, including many members of Christian churches, are active participants in the Handsome Lake religion, sometimes called the New, or the Longhouse, religion. Members are found on all the reservations, with the heaviest concentrations among the Senecas and the Onondagas. There are ten Longhouses, or religious centers, in the New York and Canadian Iroquois communities. A single organization brings together annually the members of all six nations for extended ceremonies.

Political organization also links the people of the various reservation communities. One form of organization recognizes the authority of hereditary leaders and preserves the traditions of the aboriginal League of the Iroquois, but this concept is rejected by many Senecas and others, whose councils are composed of elected representatives. Usually both kinds of organization exist on a reservation, and each has its adherents. Whichever form is followed, there is a commonly held belief that the Iroquois are a sovereign people and not subject to the U.S. government, except with regard to land matters. In that respect the authority of Congress is recognized as paramount within the framework of treaties it has ratified.

During the 1950s and later, the Mohawks, Senecas, and Tuscaroras found themselves in conflict with the New York State Power Authority and the U.S. Army Corps of Engineers over proposed power and flood-control projects. The Indians sought injunctions and brought suits to stop the government from appropriating parts of the small amount of reservation land left to them. The power authority attempted, without consulting the Indians, to take the land. In one case the Tuscaroras succeeded in blocking their efforts; other projects were eventually carried out, but only after the fight had been carried to Congress. The Kinzua Dam controversy, in which the Senecas brought suit, gained national attention and enlisted the support of many whites.

These conflicts, together with the general conditions of ethnic group assertion during the 1950s and 1960s, led to reinvigoration of the Iroquois sense of identity. In the 1960s boys and young men revived the old scalp-lock hairdo. Indian costume was revived, usually in the manner of the Sioux of the northern plains or of the Chippewa of the western Great Lakes. A cultural revival movement with a strong civil-rights orientation derived leadership chiefly from the more highly educated Iroquois. A Tuscarora named Mad Bear gained national attention in the struggle against the state power authority. Mad Bear visited widely among such Indians as the Catawba, the Miccosukee, and western tribes, demanding recognition of long-ignored Indian rights and calling attention to the federal government's mismanagement of Indian affairs. The militant movement also resulted in some new efforts to educate Iroquois adults and schoolchildren more fully in their history and cultural heritage and to project the Iroquois viewpoint on historical and current matters into the schools and before the public.

At the time of first contacts with Europeans, the Onondagas, Senecas, Mohawks, Oneidas, and Cayugas were organized into a confederacy, called by whites the League of the Iroquois, which unified the efforts of the Iroquois to take a leading role in the fur trade and to contain the French and the English. But the league had a deeper significance in Iroquois life. According to Iroquois legend, it was founded by two late-16th-century men, Deganawidah and Hiawatha, who conceived the idea of uniting the five peoples in a council of 50 sachems and proclaimed sacred principles of law unique among the Indians of the Great Lakes or of any other region. Imbued with faith in these laws, the Five Iroquois Nations became the most powerful of the Northeast Indians, destroying, absorbing, or becoming the protectors of all the tribes around them, including their Algonkian neighbors. Even large nations like the Delawares accepted their military and spiritual dominance.

Although the Iroquois became the enemies of the French and were generally supportive of the English, their real aim with respect to the Europeans was to be the dominant middlemen in the fur trade with the Indians of the North and West. In this they were successful during the early 1700s, but as friction developed between the British and their colonies, the pressures on the Iroquois from three sides became divisive. By the time of the American Revolution, the Six Nations (the Tuscaroras had joined the original five) were hopelessly split, and the league was no longer a power. During the Revolution the Oneidas and the Tuscaroras gave aid to the colonists, while the Cayugas, the Senecas, and many Mohawks were pro-British. When the English were defeated, the Americans destroyed the Seneca villages and fields and in 1783 took over the greater part of the land of the Cayugas, Mohawks, and Onondagas. Some fled to Canada when offered a large land grant there; this land became the Six Nations Reserve and served as a major center of Iroquois life into the 1970s. The New York Mohawks lost most of their population, which had dwindled to about 400, in the Canadian migration. After the Revolution the Americans sought to cultivate the able Seneca leader, Cornplanter, as leader of the New York Iroquois and gave him land grants in the old Seneca territory; these became the Allegany and the Cattaraugus reservations.

However, the spirit of the Senecas, as of the other Iroquois in New York State, had been broken. Their rebuilt villages became slums in the wilderness, disorganized and beset with drunken young men. New pressures came from the whites intent on acquiring land. In a treaty of 1797 most of the remaining Seneca land was ceded for a small sum. Without their hunting grounds, the Senecas sank into deep despair, a thoroughly disorganized society.

Meanwhile, a new force had developed within Seneca society. In 1800, Handsome Lake, one of the drunken young men of the 1790s, received a revelation that he believed pointed the way to a new life. The new way consisted of combining the old religious traditions with elements of white ways. By the time of his death in 1815, his sacred code of behavior had spread to all the Six Nations except the St. Regis Mohawks. Longhouses were built as centers for the new religion, which continues to be a major influence in Iroquois life.

As the new religion expanded, the state of New York,

spurred on by land interests and missionaries, tried to remove the Indians to the west, to facilitate the purchase of their lands. Two Iroquois factions—the Christians and the Pagans—crystallized during the early 1800s. It was a period of deep disorganization, but eventually five small pieces of land were retained, and after 1840 the code of Handsome Lake and new concepts of political organization began to point out new directions. In 1848 the Seneca Nation was formed, with a republican form of government composed of a council of 18 members, a president, and three peacemakers or judges. This organization, chartered by the federal government, helped to revitalize Iroquois political life, although the hereditary chief system of the old league persisted in the other communities. Many Iroquois attended Carlisle Indian School in Pennsylvania, another important stimulus for encouraging new contacts among the Six Nations. In 1925 Iroquois leaders joined with other Indians and whites in organizing an Indian Defense League, which sought to redress long-standing grievances and give the American public a better understanding of what Indians regarded as government injustices. This league was a mild precursor of the more vigorous militancy of the 1950s and 1960s.

THE WESTERN GREAT LAKES COUNTRY

In the 1960s more than 33,000 Indians lived in the states (Michigan, Indiana, Illinois, Wisconsin, and Minnesota) adjacent to Lakes Huron, Michigan, and Superior. This figure represents about two-thirds of the number living there when the French began to arrive in the 1500s. While most of the groups have shrunk since then, and at least one large group—the Illinois—has become extinct, the Chippewa, or Ojibwa group is considerably larger than at the time of first European contact.

Since the 1500s the number of distinct Indian groups has

decreased from 14 to 10. However, these figures mask the shifts in location of the Indian tribes of this region. Of the ten groups present in the 1960s, three—the Oneidas, the Stockbridges, and the Brothertons—were not descendants of original inhabitants of the region but had come from the east as a result of white pressures. Of the remaining seven, five represented only parts of earlier groups, larger segments having migrated or been forcibly removed from the region as a result of white settlement. Five groups had completely left the region through migration, which was voluntary only in the sense that the decision was made by Indians faced with white invasion. It is apparent, therefore, that the distribution of peoples in this region has changed radically and is a result of a history of conflict among Indians and between Indians and whites.

By states the distribution is very uneven. Illinois has no Indians outside of Chicago, and in Indiana there are only a few hundred Miamis living in scattered families. Minnesota has the largest number, with a rural population of 18,450 living outside of Minneapolis–St. Paul. Wisconsin has the second-largest Indian population with 13,927 in seven separate groups. Michigan has about 1,500 Indians.

Chippewas

As of the 1960s a total of about 36,000 Chippewas (often called Ojibwas) lived in the United States, mostly in Minnesota, and at least this many in Canada. Their distribution was as follows:

Minnesota	17,860
North Dakota	9,700
Wisconsin	4,800
Michigan	2,450
Montana	1,160

The modern U.S. total is about the same as the whole Chippewa population in 1650. By 1884 the number of Chippewas had declined to possibly 15,000, but since then it has steadily climbed, and the growth rate seemed in the 1960s to be increasing.

The Chippewas live on 15 federal reservations and in a half-dozen groups of nonreservation communities, as well as in urban neighborhoods and scattered residences in Minnesota, Illinois, and elsewhere. Most of the people on the reservations in five states, from central Montana to Michigan, identify themselves as Chippewas. The extent to which distinctions in identification are made by the people of different reservations or localities is not on record, although presumably distinctions are made, with varying degrees of importance. Separate identification within the common category of Chippewa is no doubt encouraged by their separate political organizations.

In Minnesota six of the eight reservation communities are organized into a single political-administrative unit called the Minnesota Chippewa Tribe, which maintains an elected tribal council as provided by the IRA. Other groups of communities and reservations are organized separately such as the Mississippi Band of Chippewas, which has a kind of traditional chieftainship; the Red Lake Chippewas and the reservation peoples in other states have their own tribal councils. To some extent these separate organizations are linked through the Great Lakes Inter-Tribal Council.

Considerable variation exists in the degree and kind of replacement of native cultures. In general, it was impossible to maintain the older ways of subsistence, as game disappeared, timber stands were sold or logged off, and farming on the poor reservation land became a losing enterprise. Factions formed as tribal life became disorganized, and government employees managed what economic production was possible, favoring those Chippewas they regarded as "progressive." A high proportion of Indians were on relief from the 1940s through the 1970s. On the Minnesota reservation at Red Lake, which is closed—that is, not allotted individually and closed to white intrusion—some effective tribal organization has developed. In general, however, community life is characterized by disorganization and apathy. Traditional ceremonial organization exists to varying degrees, although most people are also Catholic or Episcopalian.

A steady migration to Minnesota cities began before World War II and accelerated afterward, so that many, perhaps most, families made some degree of urban adjustment. In Minneapolis, Chippewas and Sioux were active leaders in many community development programs. Out of these urban interests grew a militant organization called the American Indian Movement (AIM), with Chippewas active in the national leadership. AIM carried out demonstrations at the BIA office in Washington, D.C., in 1972 and occupied the town of Wounded Knee, S. Dak., in 1973. Underlying these spectacular demonstrations, aimed at publicizing Indian poverty, bad government management, and legal injustices, were some vigorous and constructive achievements in Minnesota. Among these were programs to improve police protection in low-income urban neighborhoods and the introduction of a successful Indian Studies program at the University of Minnesota.

Unlike most eastern and southern Indians, the Chippewas were not forcibly removed from their homeland by the government, although whites took the greater part of their lands and depleted most of the resources. In the earlier phase of European invasion the Chippewas had expanded their territory considerably and (considering Canadian and U.S. Chippewas together) doubled their population as they sought new trapping grounds for their increasing involvement in the fur trade with the French. For example, groups of Chippewas moved from their original Lake Huron area into western Minnesota and fought the eastern Sioux for their lands. By the end of the 1700s the Chippewas had essentially taken over the territory as far west as the eastern prairies, and their population increased in these new areas as the fur trade peaked during the early 1800s. They organized themselves in small roving bands, thus breaking up the large stable communities in which they had lived during their early participation in the fur trade.

The remarkable adaptation of the Chippewas to the forest and lake country as hunters and trappers was reported to Americans in the early 19th century and became a focus of romantic interest in the Indian. The ethnologist Henry Rowe Schoolcraft reported the idyllic aspects of their life, and the poet Henry W. Longfellow, mistaking the Iroquois Hiawatha for a Chippewa, gave epic expression to the Chippewa way of life, with which a large audience in the United States and Europe became familiar.

During the 1830s, when the world fur market was suddenly curtailed, the Chippewas' economic base began to erode. In addition, the westward movement of whites put pressure on them, and in 1837 they began to make treaties, ceding large amounts of land in return for fixed annual payments over a limited time period. By the 1860s all the Chippewas were either living on very small parts of their old hunting territories or were landless wanderers within or near their old territories. The small areas to which the whites tried to confine the Chippewas were among the least usable parcels of land. As early as 1854 a treaty was forced on the Chippewas by which they agreed to assign 80 acres to each able-bodied male. In 1889, in line with national policy, the Minnesota legislature, in "an act for the relief and civilization of the Indians," provided for the division of all remaining Chippewa land into individual allotments. In 1904 arrangements were made for logging the reservation areas wherever timber remained. With little interest in farming the poor soil and without other resources, the Chippewas lived on their allotments in poverty and dependence until after World War II, when many began to move to cities.

Menominees

Numbering about 3,000 in 1976, the Menominees live on approximately 275,000 acres in northeastern Wisconsin which are in the process of being changed back to an Indian reservation, which they were before 1954. The Menominee Restoration Committee was elected by the tribe in 1974 for the express purpose of restoring the tribe's special relationship with the federal government and the reservation status of the land, which had been abolished, in accord with President Dwight Eisenhower's policy, by the Menominee Termination Act of 1954. During the 19 years when this policy was in effect, the condition of the Menominees was one of transition, and their relations with the federal government were tumultuous. The tribal treasury of $3 million was completely dissipated; their reservation became a state county; the lumber industry, which had been built up over some 50 years, was on the verge of insolvency; and Menominee land held in federal trust for 100 years was being sold piece by piece. The controlling authority of Menominee Enterprises, which had been created by the termination act to manage the Menominee lumber industry, passed from Menominee hands. To keep the shaky business solvent, parcels of land were sold along the Wolf River, the heart of the old reservation. With the loss of their land, the Menominees organized DRUMS (Determination of Rights and Unity for Menominee Stockholders), revived the tribal council, and worked for the reversal of the termination act. Action by Congress in 1973 required the transition back to earlier conditions under the direction of the Menominee Restoration Committee.

The Menominees are unusual among American Indians in that by the 1920s they had developed a successful sawmill and logging business under reservation conditions, using the profits to pay for health and education services, to provide salaries for Bureau of Indian Affairs employees, to support telephone and electric utility companies, as well as distributing profits to some tribe members and building a tribal fund. The lumber business also provided jobs for most of the group. In many other respects the native culture had been replaced, as, for example, in housing, food, and clothing. The majority are Roman Catholic, but a segment of the tribe is devoted to the so-called Drum Dance religion (*nimihetwan*), or Dancing Rite, and a few are members of the Native American church, which uses peyote in its rituals. The Menominee Algonkian language is spoken by most non-Catholics and by many Catholics. It was apparently their high degree of cultural assimilation, especially as manifested in their business operation, that led the BIA to terminate the Menominees' federal services and trust relationship.

French explorers and traders first encountered the Menominees in the late 1600s near Sault Sainte Marie and the northern end of the Michigan peninsula. They were a relatively sedentary people, who regularly harvested wild rice; their name in fact means "wild rice gatherers." As they engaged in the fur trade and became more and more dependent on trade goods, they became, like their close cultural relatives the Chippewas, more nomadic. Although by 1740 most of the Algonkian-speaking groups had been pushed out of the region, the Menominees remained in the general area of Green Bay, Wis. Generally, they supported the French and later the British and were little disturbed in hunting and gathering activities in their native territory.

However, as the Americans moved into the Northwest Territory, the usual steady erosion of Indian hunting lands took place. By an 1854 treaty they were restricted to their present 250,000-acre reservation, having ceded 9 million acres. For 20 years or more they received some rations from the U.S. government along with annual payments for the land ceded. They regarded the 1854 treaty as a final guarantee of their security and sovereignty on the reservation. The Bureau of Indian Affairs tried to introduce them to farming, but instead the Menominees developed a small-scale lumber business. By 1872 they were involved in logging under BIA supervision and had already built up a small tribal fund.

During the 1870s they held out actively against selling their timber to the "pine ring" of large lumber companies and also managed to resist having their reservation broken up into individual allotments when U.S. policy moved in that direction. Theirs was the only remaining unallotted reservation in the Great Lakes region, except for the Chippewa Red Lake reservation in Minnesota.

By 1905 the authority of the traditional headmen had been so greatly weakened that when a business committee was formed to manage the lumber business it was dominated by government employees and outside business interests. A period of extreme mismanagement ensued, with BIA employees as much or more involved than the Menominee business committee. Despite bad management and rampant fraud, the BIA did institute a sustained-yield timber production system, and during the 1920s the business prospered under its supervision. Although it was recommended in 1928 that the enterprise be given some degree of independence from government supervision, no Indians were trained for upper-level management positions. As a result, much friction developed between the elected Menominee Advisory Council and the BIA-hired management. In 1934 the Menominee tribe brought suit against the bureau for many years of mismanagement, which was settled in 1951 for $7 million.

Winnebagos

The population of the Winnebagos was between 5,000 and 6,000 in 1970. The majority, probably more than 3,000, live in Wisconsin; about 1,500 reside on a reservation in northeastern Nebraska. The remaining 1,500 are scattered in Ontario, Minnesota, and South Dakota. The two major centers of population are a large area of small communities extending from La Crosse to Wittenberg to Wisconsin Dells in central Wisconsin, and the Nebraska reservation area. There is constant visiting and communication among the widely dispersed Winnebago families.

The Wisconsin Winnebagos, who have never had a reservation in that state, live on bought or rented land; as squatters on land surrounding religious missions, as at Black River Falls; and on government land. Some are farmers, as in South Dakota and Nebraska, but the great majority are engaged in a wide range of other occupations, from local industry to seasonal harvesting of fruit and vegetables. There is some seasonal use of the traditional wigwams, which are usually covered with tarpaper rather than bark, but the majority in both Wisconsin and Nebraska live in frame houses built by the BIA. Men and women both wear ordinary American clothing, although women tend to use a distinctive style of ornament of generalized American Indian pattern.

The Winnebago language is generally spoken in the home, especially in Wisconsin. Winnebagos follow three different religious traditions—the modified traditional Medicine Lodge, or Medicine Dance, religion; the Native American church; and Christian denominations, chiefly evangelical Protestantism. The Medicine Lodge religion tends to be exclusive and its practitioners hostile to the Native American church in most communities; however, many individuals participate in all three types of religious observance. The traditional burial-house customs are practiced in many communities. Since 1969 the Winnebagos of Wisconsin have had a statewide organization under an IRA type of constitution. Their vigorous retention of traditional religion in its adapted forms, use of their language, and relatively limited cultural assimilation appear to be a result of the absence of BIA supervision. This is suggested by a comparison with the reservation people of Nebraska, where assimilation has been more extensive. It should be emphasized, however, that the Wisconsin Winnebagos were not isolated from white ways; rather, they had the opportunity to select from among white

customs to a greater extent than the reservation Winnebagos. In general, they have maintained, with modifica-
tions, basic elements of their native world view and customs
wherever they have lived.

The history of the Winnebagos might suggest that their
contacts would have been conducive to breakdown and disorganization of their culture. A Siouan tribe in respect to
language, they were wedged between the Algonkian-speaking Menominees and the Sauk and Fox tribes when French
explorers entering the central Great Lakes region encountered them about 1634. Through a corridor to the south, they
maintained communication with the Siouan tribes of the
Mississippi Valley region, such as the Iowa and Omaha.
Fighting broke out in the 1670s and 1680s among the Chippewas, Foxes, Sauks, the French, and others in their vicinity, which was very disruptive to the Winnebago lifestyle. In
1671 they were seriously defeated by the Illinois and seem to
have been reduced from about 4,000 to a single village. Their
numbers increased greatly during the following century,
and in 1806 they were reported to be living in seven large
villages. Their numbers were reduced again during the early
19th century as a result of war with Chippewas and with the
Americans. Some 40 Winnebagos died in the Shawnee chief
Tecumseh's unsuccessful war against the Americans, after
which the tribe sought peace with the Americans. Yielding
to increasing American pressures, they made a series of treaties between 1816 and 1855 in which they ultimately ceded
all their lands east of the Mississippi River and then those
lands west of the river granted by the United States. They
were shunted first to a neutral ground in Iowa, then successively to reservations in Minnesota, South Dakota, and finally Nebraska, where the United States bought for them
half of the reservation guaranteed to the Omahas. With
every shift of location, each of which broke the prior treaty,
some Winnebagos were left behind. Soldiers tried to force
them to stay on the Minnesota and South Dakota reservations, but with little success. By the time the Nebraska reser-

vation was established in 1865, after 40 years of being moved about, 1,700 Winnebagos had settled in that state. There were still 860 in Wisconsin, as well as others scattered along the way.

In 1874 the government finally gave up in its efforts to keep them from returning to Wisconsin, but no reservation was established there. Instead, 40-acre homesteads, tax-free for 20 years, were granted to each family head who could be located among the 900 or so Winnebagos who had outlasted the government's 50-year effort to move them out of Wisconsin. Meanwhile, the government made individual allotments to the Winnebagos who remained on the Nebraska reservation; an Indian agent continued to supervise their affairs, even though the reservation was no longer owned collectively. Many farmed and proceeded generally on a path of cultural assimilation.

The Wisconsin Winnebagos remain a powerful influence on the reservation people. Besides vitalizing the Medicine Bundle religion of their ancient tradition and contributing to its continuation among some reservation Winnebagos, the Wisconsin group became prominent in the Peyote cult when it began to diffuse from the southern Plains Indians in 1908, and they encouraged the ritual among the Nebraska Winnebagos.

Other Indians of the western Great Lakes are the Forest Potawatomis and Ottawas of Michigan, the Brothertons, Stockbridges, Oneidas, and Potawatomis of Wisconsin, and the Miamis of Indiana.

THE MISSISSIPPI VALLEY

In the central and lower Mississippi Valley region, the original native peoples were almost entirely exterminated or driven out by invading whites and other Indians: Iowa, Missouri, Arkansas, and Mississippi were without Indians by the late 19th century. Only Louisiana retained some of the variety of original Indian inhabitants, although all except the Houma, much intermixed with French, were reduced to a tiny fraction of their former numbers; some groups were entirely extinguished.

During the 1900s the Fox and the Choctaws returned to Iowa and Mississippi, respectively, and became permanent residents. One group of Choctaws accepted a reservation, but others live in independent communities. A small Indian population, almost all on federal reservations, lives in Nebraska and Kansas. In the 1960s the total Indian population of this western edge of the Mississippi Valley, together with the Foxes of central Iowa, was between 6,000 and 7,000; the returned Choctaws in Mississippi numbered about 2,600, and the Indian population of Louisiana was 2,980. This total population for the region, about 11,750, is approximately one-fifth of the population that existed in about the same area at the time of initial contacts with whites. There were possibly about the same number of distinct groups—15 to 20—in the 1960s as during the early phases of contact, but not an exact correspondence. Five of the groups came from the western Great Lakes region, pushed out of their homeland by the pressures of European settlement and forced migration. The main bodies of two of these tribes—Chippewas and Winnebagos—are still in their Great Lakes homelands; the Kickapoos and the Sauks and Foxes were completely displaced. The Potawatomis of Kansas represent only one important division of that tribe, the others being located in Michigan, Wisconsin, and Oklahoma.

Potawatomis

By the 1970s there were about 6,000 Potawatomis in the United States, distributed in four states as follows:

Michigan (3 communities)	450
Wisconsin (2 communities)	400
Kansas (1 U.S. reservation)	2,000
Oklahoma (former reservation)	3,000
	5,850

In addition, a few Potawatomis live in Ontario and in various urban centers. They regard themselves as three distinct groups: the Forest Potawatomi of Michigan and Wisconsin, the Prairie Band of Potawatomi of Kansas, and the Citizen Potawatomi of Oklahoma.

On the Kansas reservation a core of long-time, extremely conservative residents, the Prairie Band, successfully resisted having their land broken into allotments, rejected organizing under the IRA, and through a business committee won a $5 million claim before the Indian Claims Commission. As the money became available in the 1950s, the tribal roll increased from 500 to 2,000. Those who returned to the reservation, who had moved away and dissociated themselves from tribal affairs prior to the 1930s, engaged in a struggle for adoption of a constitution and a tribal council. They were finally successful in 1961, but their conflict with the conservatives continues to dominate local politics. Most of the conservative faction never became Christians, maintaining active participation in native religious life focused around the Dream Dance, the Medicine Dance, or the Native American church, and they continue to speak the Potawatomi language. The others on the Prairie Band tribal roll are Christian and in occupation, dress, and other ways are very much assimilated.

The 3,000 Citizen Potawatomis of Oklahoma are even more assimilated, whereas the descendants of the Forest Band in the Great Lakes region are generally less so. Most live under a tribal council government but are otherwise like rural whites of the area. The Prairie Potawatomi have been extremely active in pan-Indian pow-wows and in the militant Indian movements of the 1960s.

The Potawatomis claim as their homeland a region of the north shore of Lake Huron, where they were associated with Ottawas and Chippewas at the beginning of the white invasions. They then moved south and by the end of the 18th century dominated the Indians of the Illinois area. Their resistance to white encroachment was sporadic and not well organized, and they steadily ceded lands during the early 19th century. In the Treaty of Chicago of 1833, they ceded 5 million acres in Illinois and Indiana and moved across the Mississippi, where they settled first in Iowa, then Missouri, and later in Kansas. Some Potawatomis remained behind in scattered groups and became known as the Forest Band of Ontario, Wisconsin, and Michigan.

A federal reservation was established in northeastern Kansas where the Potawatomis of the United Band of Potawatomis, Chippewas, and Ottawas (the Prairie Band) were forced to settle, as were a group of very assimilated Potawatomis called the Mission Band. A serious schism developed in the 1860s over the issue of accepting individual allotments of land, a plan pushed by whites in an effort to break up the tribal organization and hasten individual cultural assimilation. When the General Allotment Act of 1887 was passed, a determined segment of Potawatomis continued to oppose allotment, and the majority of the Prairie Band were never forced to accept it. Descendants of the Mission Band and others, who were becoming white-oriented, accepted allotment and U.S. citizenship and became individual farmers. This group, calling themselves the Citizen Potawatomis, was anxious to separate from the conservatives, so they sold their allotments and established a reservation in Oklahoma. That reservation, too, was eventually broken up into allotments; they continue to live there, generally prospering as farmers and livestock raisers. In 1948 they organized as the Citizen Band of Potawatomi Indians of Oklahoma with a charter from the state.

About 1876 the Prairie Potawatomis began to share, along with the Forest Band, the Menominees, and the Winnebagos, in a new religious revelation. Brought by a Sioux woman, the Dream Dance, as it was called, offered an alternative to the many forms of Christianity. The chief spirits of the new religion were the traditional supernaturals in whom they had believed and some newer prophets, who spoke in the traditional Indian languages but met the Indians' changing needs with regard to health and the ordering of experience. The Dream Dance involved no sweeping changes but was part of a process of continuing vitalization of the traditional forms.

Foxes

In the 1970s there were between 500 and 600 Fox Indians living on 2,800 acres near Tama, Iowa. Their situation is unusual in that this land is not a reservation (it was purchased during the 19th century and held in federal trust), but the BIA does have some role in their lives. They lease another 520 acres to whites, the rent going toward payment of taxes on the main tract.

From the early 18th century the Foxes were closely associated with the Sauk, or Sac, Indians of the upper Great Lakes area, and by the 20th century the Foxes had largely absorbed their allies. There are 130 Sauk and Fox Indians living on a small reservation in eastern Nebraska and Kansas and another 1,000 on a reservation in central Oklahoma. The Oklahoma reservation, it is claimed, is inhabited chiefly by Sauk rather than Fox Indians, but the family lines are so mixed that no clear determination can be made. Since about the 1830s no separate listing of the two groups has been made.

The Foxes (Meskwaki in their own language) are the only Indian group now living in Iowa, which was the temporary residence of a dozen different tribes during the 18th and early 19th centuries. The Foxes are farmers, but they also work in industry and for non-Indian farmers. Frame houses have been used since 1902, when all the village dwellings were burned by order of Iowa health authorities in order to stop a raging smallpox epidemic. When they rebuilt, they dispersed in the manner of American farmers, and they continue to maintain this pattern today. They also use Algonkian wigwams and for certain religious ceremonies erect canvas-covered tipis. Most families have automobiles and many use tractors in their farming.

In the 1960s nearly one-third of the Tama community spoke only the Fox language, and some persons could read and write using the Algonkian syllabary. Two-thirds were bilingual in English and Fox. Very few Foxes participate in Christian religious churches, and nearly all are members of the medicine societies, whose religious rites revolve around sacred medicine bundles. Some are active in the Native American church, and others practice the Drum Dance rites introduced by Potawatomis, some of whom lived in the Fox community. In addition, there is another religion called the Singing-Around Society, introduced by Wisconsin Indians.

An elected council, organized somewhat along the lines of the IRA prescription, has been in existence since 1937. There are two recognized factions in the community, often thought of as antiwhite and prowhite, but this is an oversimplification. The community supports an elementary school with some aid from the federal government and from non-Indian organizations. Community effort is totally organized in the annual pow-wow, a public spectacle that draws thousands of whites, Indians, and tourists and makes use of the pan-Indian pageantry common at pow-wows, including the Hiawatha and Minnehaha symbols that are widespread throughout the eastern United States. Three sacred bundle feasts and four Drum Dance ceremonies take place each year.

During early French exploration of the Great Lakes area, the Foxes lived on the west side of Lake Michigan, and the Sauks lived immediately to the north of them, west of Green Bay. After a brief friendly traffic with French traders and missionaries, the Foxes became deeply hostile to the French and gained their enmity by interfering, somewhat successfully, with French trade with other Indians. By the late 1720s the French had launched a campaign to exterminate the Foxes, enlisting Winnebagos, Ottawas, Chippewas, and Menominees against them, and in 1730 they almost succeeded. The remnant of the Foxes was befriended by the Sauks, and both groups allied with the Kickapoos in a confederacy with other tribes of the Great Lakes region. However, the fact that the Foxes were friendly with the Iroquois made them enemies of the northern Great Lakes tribes. Foxes played a small role in Ottawa chief Pontiac's 1763 uprising and later aided Tecumseh's great effort to unite the Algonkian-speaking nations against the Americans during the War of 1812. Their loyalty shifted several times, but by the beginning of the 19th century the Foxes had sided with Spain and Britain against the Americans. In 1804 some chiefs of the Sauk and Fox tribes made a treaty, not authorized by the responsible tribal authorities, ceding to the Americans all their lands on both sides of the Mississippi. The Americans held to the treaty, which became a point of serious conflict with the Foxes. As pressures for Indian removal grew, Black Hawk (1767–1838), an elderly Sauk war leader in Illinois, mounted a short-lived and unsuccessful resistance against the Illinois militia and other troops, called the Black Hawk War, in 1832. After the village was burned, the crops destroyed, and Black Hawk taken prisoner, leadership passed to another Sauk, Keokuk (c. 1790–1848), who sought to cooperate with the Americans.

Under his rule the Sauk and Fox Indians, like other Great Lakes tribes, were pushed from one place to another, and treaties with them were broken repeatedly. First they were put on a reservation in Iowa, then in Kansas, and then in Oklahoma. The main body went to Oklahoma, where in 1891 their land was individually allotted. Some Foxes returned to the Iowa area and bought 80 acres of land. They steadily added more land, paid for with the annuities from other land cessions. Their Iowa land was under state trust until 1895, when the federal government assumed responsibility. They became tax-paying citizens of Iowa, little interfered with by either missionary groups or federal employees. Their continuing interest in the Meskwaki language and the several native American religions in which they participate indicate their cultural independence.

The other branch of the Sauk and Fox Indians in Oklahoma moved toward cultural assimilation. Since allotment they have had no collectively owned land and have been supervised in various ways by the Bureau of Indian Affairs. A BIA boarding school was maintained on their land after 1872. In 1885 they organized as the Sac and Fox Nation under a written constitution and established tribal courts. In 1936 they reorganized, retaining very much the old political structure but under the provisions of the Oklahoma Indian Welfare Act. Most are Methodists or Baptists. A very few still speak the Algonkian languages, as well as English.

Kickapoos

Kickapoo history is in many respects the most remarkable of all the Indian histories in the United States. Some of them have maintained the major elements of their aboriginal way of life through 350 years of the most varied social and physical conditions experienced by an Indian group. They moved from their woodland home near the Great Lakes in northern Wisconsin into the prairies and then to the progressively more arid regions from Indian Territory to Coahuila in northern Mexico. They have survived under successive conditions of nearly constant warfare, brief government supervision, and then complete independence. They have been subjected to removals and to reservation life. Yet even without a long-sustained and stable land base, many kept their traditional ways.

By the 1960s they were settled in three major locations, the northernmost some 1,500 miles from the southernmost—in Kansas 400 live on a federal reservation; in Oklahoma there are 300 in an independent village; and in Coahuila, Mexico there are 400. The more than 1,100 Kickapoos of the 1960s were slightly more than one-half the number encountered by Europeans 300 years earlier. Their population declined from about 2,000 in the mid-19th century.

The way of life of the modern Kickapoos of Coahuila closely resembles that of the 17th century with respect to housing (wigwams), hunting ways, religion, Algonkian language, community structure, and family life. On the other hand, the Kansas reservation community, called the Prairie Band, is like a community of American farmers, with frame houses, modern, successful farming methods, and membership in the Baptist or Methodist church; however, most members of Christian churches also follow the religious practices prescribed by the 19th-century prophet Kennekuk. They have a representative government modeled according to the IRA plan.

In Oklahoma the Kickapoos' ways vary from the extreme conservatism of the Mexican group, to those of the Kansas Kickapoos, but the majority are conservative. Their houses are still built on the plan of the bark houses of the Great Lakes Algonkians but are now covered with mats and canvas. In their farming they use the old hand tools along with recently adopted modern farm implements. Their religion is of the old Manitou type, centering around sacred bundles and requiring lengthy ceremonials at New Year and at the Green Corn rituals in the summer.

The Kickapoo cultural conservatism has been maintained in spite of extreme changes in their conditions. When they were first known to whites in northern Wisconsin, they were a farming and hunting people. Their religious, family, and other customs were similar to those of the Foxes and Potawatomis. The Kickapoos' early contacts with the French led to permanent hostility, as they held the French responsible for stimulating Sioux raids into their country from the west and Iroquois raids from the east. The Kickapoos turned to warfare as a major pursuit, organizing a confederacy with the Sauk, Fox, and Forest Potawatomi tribes. They supported

Pontiac in his abortive effort to eliminate the whites in 1763 and later, in the early 1800s strongly supported the Shawnee prophet Tenskwatawa and Tecumseh. They thus established themselves as active opponents of the Americans.

The Kickapoos had begun to move westward, pushed by the tribes moving into the Great Lakes area, even before the defeats of 1811–1812. Some had been forced out of Wisconsin into Illinois and ranged farther west as early as the last quarter of the 18th century. Along with other displaced peoples, like the Delawares, the Shawnees, and some Mississippi Valley tribes, they became mercenary soldiers for the Spaniards. They protected the Spanish settlements from the Chickasaws and later from the Osages of the Missouri River region. Between 1819 and the 1880s the Kickapoos were referred to as "the lords of the middle border," an appellation that recognized their excellent fighting abilities.

At the end of the 18th century those who remained in the east participated in the near extermination of the Illinois and other tribes of the area, then established villages in the former Illinois territory. This occurred at the very time when Americans were moving in large numbers into the virgin farmland of the area, which resulted in constant clashes. After the defeat of Tecumseh and subsequent unsuccessful fighting by the Kickapoos, they signed a treaty in 1819. They agreed to cede all their land in Illinois and Indiana and to move across the Mississippi into what became Missouri. Many small bands resisted removal, but eventually all went to western Missouri, where villages had already been established by the mercenary Kickapoos and their relatives along the Osage River. By 1824 there were 2,200 Kickapoos reported there, most of the tribe. About this time a prophet appeared among the Kickapoos, a man named Kennekuk, who had been a war chief. His vision called for peace, a cessation of opposition to the Americans and peace with other Indians. His teaching was wholly inconsistent with the adopted lifestyle of the majority of Kickapoos, but he promptly gained several hundred adherents. He advocated settling down to a farming life while adhering to some of their traditional religious beliefs and rituals.

The majority continued their border warfare, and during the 1820s they redoubled their war activities; the passion for raiding that had characterized their early resistance to the French was renewed against the Osages of the Missouri basin and against the steadily advancing settlers. Another segment of the tribe had settled permanently in Spanish Territory, in what was shortly to become Texas. During 1815–1817 this group joined a Cherokee leader from Arkansas, Chief Bowles, who had made an arrangement with the Spaniards to settle on the Sabine River in Texas territory, where, along with Delawares and Shawnees, they became Spanish citizens. They were soon joined by Kickapoos from the north.

In 1832, Missouri Kickapoos, seeking land farther west, made a treaty with the Americans for a reservation in Kansas near Fort Leavenworth. Some 700 followers of Kennekuk, along with a strongly anti-American segment, moved to the Kansas reservation in 1833, where the prophet and his followers settled down permanently. Some of the opposing faction left in 1837 to join the Texas Kickapoos. Meanwhile, the Republic of Texas had been established, and in 1839 the Texans, who were deeply hostile to Indians, forced the Texas Kickapoos out of the republic. Some went north into what had become Indian Territory; some Kickapoos and others moved south into Mexico, where they established a community on the Rio Grande. Although the Kickapoos who went north to Indian Territory had no formal relationship with the U.S. government, having lived outside the country for years, they established themselves west of the Chickasaw Nation and from there regularly raided the Texans, the Chickasaws, and other Indians. They numbered at this time about 1,200 and regarded themselves as being at war with the Republic of Texas, which had ousted them from villages they had established long before the republic was founded. Faced with the growing hostility of other Indians moving into Indian

Territory, the Kickapoos accepted a friendly invitation to settle in the Creek Nation and provide protection from other raiding "wild tribes." In 1842 the Texans changed their approach and sought the protective assistance of the Kickapoos and invited them to return to Texas, where they reestablished their villages along the Brazos and the Canadian rivers, becoming specialized as hunters, traders, and soldiers defending the Creeks against attacks.

With the outbreak of the Civil War, the Kickapoos moved north into Kansas in an effort to escape the pressure to ally themselves with the Confederacy. Some went first to the Kansas reservation but found themselves unable to live in harmony with the steadily assimilating northern group descended from Kennekuk's disciples. In 1865 all the southern Kickapoos, after raiding the Cherokees, Creeks, and others who had gone over to the Confederacy, trekked to Mexico, taking up residence in Coahuila, at the invitation of the Mexican government. There in Nacimiento they acted as a buffer between the Mexicans and the constantly raiding Comanches and Lipan Apaches—a situation they enjoyed. However, between 1865 and 1872 they also raided Texas, making serious inroads into the southern settlements.

In an effort to make life safer for the Texans, the United States tried to force the Mexican Kickapoos to return across the border by, among other tactics, raiding into Coahuila, destroying the Kickapoo village, killing women and children, and taking 40 women and children hostage. Eventually, after much negotiation, 350, or about one-half the Mexican Kickapoo community agreed to follow their captive relatives to Indian Territory; 400 remained in Coahuila. From 1874 on, a community of some 450 Kickapoos existed in Indian Territory and remained after the state of Oklahoma was established.

The Kickapoos in Indian Territory maintained themselves very much as they had wherever they had lived before. In large measure they kept control of their own affairs. They chose their own location near the Sac and Fox, refusing to accept the location chosen for them by the BIA because it was next to their enemies, the Osages. They built their traditional bark or mat-covered houses, refused to send their children to school, maintained vigorously their old religious ceremonies and beliefs, rejected white medical treatment, hunted (on Chickasaw lands) in their old destructive manner, spoke their own language, and devoted much time to visiting and to religious life. Each time BIA employees attempted to force cultural assimilation programs on them, the Kickapoos threatened to return to Mexico, but they accepted rations and farming tools as their due. When the government program for individual allotment reached its peak about 1895, nearly all the Kickapoos refused to accept it. When it was forced on them and surplus lands were opened to white settlement, some returned to Mexico, where the Coahuila settlement continued to thrive. Some aspects of allotment in Oklahoma were delayed until 1915 because of a complex case of fraud by an agent of the Kickapoos. Similarly, when allotment was pushed on the Kansas reservation, there was fraud involving the government Indian agents, as a railroad company sought to swindle the Indians out of a large portion of the reservation lands. Most Kansas Kickapoos nevertheless accepted the government program, continued to farm, and became culturally very much like their neighbors.

Omahas and Poncas

Besides the Winnebagos, two other surviving Indian groups —the Omahas and the Poncas—live along the Missouri River in Nebraska, on the western margin of the Mississippi Valley. Unlike the Winnebagos, who are of Great Lakes origin, the Omahas and Poncas are related to the southern Plains Indians in their way of life. During the previous centuries the two tribes were closely associated in the region of Nebraska where their 20th-century reservations were ultimately established. The main body of Poncas is in Oklahoma, but some 450 live intermingled with Santee Sioux on a reservation on the Missouri River in northeastern Nebraska. The remaining Omahas, about 2,000 in 1960, live on a reservation in eastern Nebraska that adjoins the Winnebago reservation on the south.

The Omahas live on individually held land among white farmers and stock raisers whose land was formerly part of the reservation. There is thus some intermingling of whites and Indians in the area, but the Omahas are separate from the white society in most ways. They are classified as Indians by the government and therefore receive medical and educational assistance for which whites are not eligible, and to some degree they are supervised by the BIA. Under the provisions of the IRA, the Omahas organized a tribal council that has some jurisdiction over the land they still hold in common (by tribal title) and that organizes the annual camp ceremony. The council has no taxation power or other governmental functions.

More than 90 percent of the Omahas under the age of 40 speak English. Many speak Omaha as well, but there is an apparent trend toward the loss of the Siouan language. They dress much like the surrounding whites, the men having adopted the cattlemen's large Stetson hats. Families live in frame houses, and the children attend public school. The men engage in a variety of occupations, but most residents derive a large part of their income from leasing farm or range lands to whites. Most profess to be Presbyterians, but few attend church with any regularity. Some families are active Mormons. Nearly all the Omahas participate to some degree in the Native American church, and there is much interest in intertribal pow-wows, which Omaha dance groups attend.

The Omahas suffered relatively little displacement in the course of their contacts with whites, in contrast with most of the peoples east of the Mississippi. Their present location is a small portion of the land where they built villages before the invasion by whites. They were an agricultural people, who supplemented their intensive farming with annual buffalo hunts in the plains to the west and north. They lived in relatively dense village communities, where related families lived together in large earth lodges. The Omahas never developed coup-counting warfare or the total dependence on the buffalo that characterized other tribes farther west and north. They retained many woodland tribal traditions, such as the Medicine Bundle religion and the curing societies, including the Midewiwin, which was characteristic of the Indians to the northeast. They also sought visions for supernatural inspiration.

The Omahas had little contact with French fur traders, their earliest important contacts being with Anglo-Americans at the beginning of their push beyond the Mississippi River. They remained friendly to the Americans and, partly as a result, were never removed wholly from their aboriginal territory. In 1850 they ceded nearly all of their land to the United States and were assigned a reservation about twice the size of their modern land. By the 1890s half of it had been taken from them, despite the 1850 treaty, to provide a reservation for the Winnebagos, and their reservation was entirely allotted, with the surplus opened for white settlement.

From 1850 the Omahas were the object of cultural assimilation programs by both the Presbyterian church and the Bureau of Indian Affairs. They yielded with little overt resistance, settled down to live in the frame houses provided, began to wear "citizens' clothes," sent their children to school, became nominal Presbyterians, and gave up their council of hereditary chiefs for BIA supervision.

By the early 1900s they seemed on the verge of thorough social and cultural assimilation, but their special status as American Indians under government supervision encouraged other cultural processes. During the 20th century, instead of wholly becoming farmers, they found it possible to make a living by leasing their land to whites, which allowed them to nurture many other interests, such as ceremonial dances, singing, and gambling. Although they did some farming, they developed a certain degree of contempt for the daily labor involved. At the same time the new Native American church was introduced, probably by Potawatomis and Winnebagos, and filled important needs. This religious rite, focusing on the use of peyote and the visions it induced, embodied many traditional Indian concepts and rites and therefore appealed to people who were losing their traditional cultural ways under the pressures for assimilation. The peyote cult became the dominant religious interest of the Omahas. Through it, many of the traditional religious practices including curing societies and sacred bundles, were revived and integrated with new elements such as funeral rites.

A kind of reservation culture has developed. Even as the Native American church declined among them during the 1930s, new cultural interests were fostered by increasing contact with other Indians. Various pan-Indian activities, as in the pow-wow circuits, have claimed their interest and consumed much time.

Other Indians living in the lower Mississippi Valley in the 1970s were: Alabamas, Atakapas, Biloxis, Chitamachas, Coushattas, Iowas, Munsee-Chippewas, and Tunicas.

THE CRUCIBLE OF OKLAHOMA

In the 1970s at least 39 different Indian ethnic groups lived in Oklahoma—the greatest number in any state of the United States. The reason for the large number of distinct peoples was the U.S. government's attempt during the mid-19th century to concentrate all Indians east of the Mississippi River and many from the Great Plains into the small compass of Indian Territory, which later became Oklahoma. Before that time, the area contained no more than four Indian tribes, which ranged widely beyond the limits of what became Indian Territory. The Indian population of the state is not easy to estimate, but it is somewhere in the neighborhood of

165,000, as contrasted with less than 10,000 before removal. Thus in Oklahoma there has been a sixteen-fold increase in the Indian population during about 150 years, and there are more than nine times as many tribes.

Delawares

In 1970 nearly 8,000 persons in the United States identified themselves as of Delaware descent, although perhaps less than 2,000 live in identifiable Delaware communities. Two Delaware communities in Oklahoma—one in the northeast near Bartlesville, with a population of about 1,350, and one in the southwest near Anadarko with no more than 200— constitute the main body of the tribe, which in 350 years has migrated across the country from the Atlantic coast to Texas and Oklahoma.

The Delawares of Oklahoma live like American white rural and urban people, using the same kinds of houses, clothing, tools, and farm implements. The Delaware language is not used in the home, although a few individuals have culti- vated a knowledge of the tongue. Most Delawares are Chris- tian, Baptists predominating, but some are members of the Native American church, especially in the Anadarko com- munity. The native Delaware Big House religion has not been practiced for half a century, and the sacred carvings that characterized the Big House ceremonial building have been relegated to a museum. Although cultural replacement is far advanced, a strong sense of Delaware identity exists in both the Anadarko and the Bartlesville groups. The latter have an elected Delaware Tribal Business Committee, which represents the group in all business dealings, including those with the Indian Claims Commission, and maintains a corporate existence for the tribe. A similar but separate orga- nization exists among the Anadarko Delawares, consisting of a committee of six called the Delaware Tribe of Western Oklahoma.

There are other groups of Delaware descent in the United

States. In Wisconsin a group calling themselves the Brothertons or Brotherton Indians, deriving their name from a town in New Jersey, numbers about 1,500. Although they do not usually call themselves Delawares, the nucleus from which they are descended had the same eastern United States origin as the Oklahoma Delawares. In Wisconsin there is another group of less than 500, known as the Stockbridge Indians, whose origin is more diverse than the Brothertons but includes some Delawares. Both the Brothertons and the Stockbridges have reservations. There is also a nonreservation community in Ontario of about 350 Delawares. Thus, there are 4,000 people living in Delaware communities in the United States, but less than half of these claim a simple Delaware identity. The figure of 8,000 mentioned above can best be clarified through a recounting of Delaware history.

The Delawares are descended from one of the largest Algonkian-speaking groups of the Atlantic coast. When the Dutch first settled in their country in 1642, there were between 8,000 and 12,000 speakers of their language. Their tribal name was Lenni Lenape, although they accepted their current designation from the name of the Englishman who administered their tribal area in the early colonial period. At that time they inhabited what is now New Jersey, southeastern Pennsylvania, northern and central Delaware, and northeastern Maryland. They did not live as a single organized tribe; rather they were groups of independent villages, each with a hereditary headman. As with the other Indians of the northern Atlantic seaboard, friendly relations with Europeans turned hostile as pressure on them increased. The Delawares were subordinated politically to the Iroquois, who exacted tribute from them and prohibited them from taking up arms. This made them especially easy to dominate and push from their lands, which the English did after 1664, when they took over political control of the region.

Immediately after the English takeover, the Delaware population began a steep decline, and by the end of the 1600s they were reduced by half. Much Delaware land was sold during the administration of William Penn, and by 1720 they were concentrated in three groups west of the Delaware River. In 1742 the Iroquois ordered the Delawares to move farther west to the Susquehanna Valley, where two large settlements of Shawnees and other displaced peoples under Iroquois domination were being established. For the Iroquois these communities served as a buffer against British settlement in the Southeast. The Delawares took up residence in the Wyoming Valley and vicinity in Pennsylvania, where they remained for some 25 years. Eventually, some Delawares began to drift westward, and two branches of the nation developed, an Ohio group under an hereditary chief named Shingas and a Susquehanna group under a nonhereditary chief named Teedyuscung. Both men supported the Iroquois effort to stay neutral in the French-British rivalry for control of the fur trade. Ultimately in 1765 and the next few years, the Iroquois sold their allies' land in Pennsylvania, leaving the Delawares landless.

Three thousand moved west into Ohio and settled along the Muskingum River, while others went north through Iroquois country to Ontario. A small community in an area called Brotherton, N.J., was placed on a reservation and refused to go west at the urging of the Ohio Delawares. Much later, in 1802, the Brotherton Indians sold their reservation and moved to Wisconsin, where they now live.

When the Revolution broke out, the Delawares in Ohio consisted of two very distinct factions—the Christians and the non-Christians—who lived in separate communities but continued to identify and associate with each other. Moravian missionaries who were active in the settlements put their language in written form and encouraged the Indians to read and write. A Delaware leader called White Eyes sought to persuade the Americans to create a 14th state for all Indians. Another Delaware leader—Captain Pipe—opposed the Americans and influenced all the Delawares to fight against them. The result was a systematic massacre by American militia of the major Delaware Christian community in 1782. By treaties in 1785 and 1795, the Delawares lost all the land rights given to them by the Wyandot Indians in Ohio and were forced west.

The Miamis invited the Delawares to settle with them in their territory along the Wabash River, and by 1801 there were 11 Delaware villages near what is now Muncie, Ind. Some Delawares moved farther west to southeastern Missouri, then to Arkansas, and then Texas, where they became mercenaries for the Spaniards, fighting the Comanches.

Meanwhile, a nativist movement developed among the Delawares in Indiana. Reacting against the breaking of treaties by Americans, they rejected white ways by, for example, going back to bark houses and refusing to use plows. But the movement was short-lived. Yielding to the ever-mounting pressures, they ceded all rights to their Indiana land in 1818 and two years later moved across the Mississippi River into Missouri. Immediately they were thrown into conflict with the Osages, on whose land they and other eastern Indians had settled. After years of great difficulty, they made a new treaty with the United States in 1829, which granted them 2 million acres in Kansas along with an outlet corridor to the plains for buffalo hunting.

Here the Delawares lived for 38 years, most farming, but a few serving as mercenaries for the United States in the costly struggle to conquer the Seminoles in Florida. They formulated a constitution and a set of tribal laws in an effort to curb the lawlessness that had grown among them. In 1860 most of their land in Kansas was allotted; by 1866, after years of harassment by settlers, railroad company agents, and their own government agents, they left Kansas and settled down in Indian Territory on a tract of land on the eastern margin of the Cherokee Nation. In their treaty with the Cherokees, negotiated before they left Kansas, they had agreed to assume all the rights and obligations of Cherokee citizens. Delawares were elected to the Cherokee National Council. Two divisions developed, the so-called modernists, who were predominantly Baptists, and the traditionalists,

who practiced the Big House native religion. There was a revival of native crafts and old ways of hunting.

When allotments in Indian Territory were forced in the
1890s, there were about 1,000 Delawares. Some were prominent in the founding of the Native American church, based
on peyote ceremonialism, into which Delaware ritual was
incorporated. When the Indian Claims Commission was
created in 1946 the Delawares presented claims for land they
had lost in Ohio, Indiana, Missouri, and Kansas and were
awarded about $13 million in compensation. Eligibility to
share in these benefits was based on relationship with persons listed on the tribal roll of 1867, when departures for
Kansas had begun. With this incentive, 7,926 individuals
had established eligibility by 1970. The new roll included
hundreds of Delawares who no longer lived in Delaware
communities, many of whom had remained in one of the
areas through which the group had passed in its long jour-
ney.

Cherokees

Population estimates for the Cherokees in Oklahoma vary
widely, indicating the considerable cultural diversity among
them and the varying definitions of ethnic identity. The estimates during the period 1960–1970 ranged from 75,000
down to about 16,000. A figure for 1950 of about 47,000 is
probably the best approximation in terms of the criterion
employed here, namely, self-identification. The 1960 census
figure was 25,600, while the much higher estimate of 75,000
that same year represents the total number having legal status as Cherokees through tribal roll eligibility. The low figure of 16,000 is a careful estimate of the culturally most
conservative Cherokees in the area of heaviest rural
concentration in northeastern Oklahoma, where they constitute a considerable percentage of the total population in six
counties.

Most Cherokees live in Oklahoma, both in rural areas of

the northeast and in cities and towns all over the state. They vary greatly in culture; for more than a century they have been in the vanguard of what most Americans call civilization in Indian Territory and Oklahoma, but they also live in isolated communities in the hilly eastern part of the state under circumstances most Americans would consider backward. By the 1970s they were established in a wide range of occupations, from business executives to fishermen and industrial workers.

Most Cherokees are Baptists or Methodists, but many also participate in forms of the native Cherokee religions as practiced by the United Keetoowah Band, the Keetoowah Society, the Nighthawk Keetoowahs, the Seven Clans Society, and the Four Mothers Society. These groups meet in rural areas and some towns and do not exclude members of Christian churches. The Native American church has very few adherents among Cherokees.

Tribal government consists of a principal chief appointed by the president of the United States and an advisory cabinet representing the Cherokee Nation and serving as the channel for various federal economic development programs. The tribal government maintains a Cherokee National Fund, has established a cultural center in Tahlequah that annually produces the drama, *The Trail of Tears*, employs a legal staff to prosecute Cherokee claims before the Indian Claims Commission, and maintains an arts and crafts development program, a national archives, and a Cherokee National Museum. There is also a newspaper, the *Cherokee Nation News*, and other enterprises. An organization known as the Elected Community Representatives was established in the 1970s to democratize the tribal organization through popular elections.

During the early 19th century the Cherokees came to think of themselves as full-bloods and mixed-bloods. Although by 1970 the terms had no significance genetically, they did refer to meaningful cultural divisions. The term full-blood refers to rural dwellers, whose way of life is chiefly farming and hunting, whose attitude toward urban lifestyles is conservative and disapproving, and who maintain the Cherokee language as a functional part of their lives. The term is also sometimes applied to urbanized individuals whose interest in Cherokee native traditions intensified during the 1950s and 1960s, but who are not necessarily accepted as full-bloods by the other full-bloods.

The Cherokees are an Iroquoian-speaking tribe that was never anything but the enemy of the Iroquois. They helped drive the Tuscaroras out of North Carolina in 1711 when that tribe sought the protection of the Iroquois League. Europeans encountered the Cherokees when they were living in what became eastern Kentucky and Tennessee and western North and South Carolina. During the early period of English settlement, they were pushed southwest, and by the early 19th century, as a result of the pressure of American settlers, they had moved into northern Georgia as well. By this time they had divided into three groups: the most conservative group remained in the southern Appalachian Mountains and became the nucleus of the 20th-century Eastern Band of Cherokees; another group voluntarily moved west of the Mississippi, settled in Arkansas, and was spoken of as the Western Band; the main body of Cherokees concentrated in northern Georgia, moving their old town center of Echota there and calling it New Echota.

In the first third of the 19th century, the Georgia Cherokees initiated profound changes in their mode of life, including organizing a political structure similar to that of the United States, which led to their classification by whites as a civilized tribe. They wrote a constitution establishing them as the Cherokee Nation and a body of laws, making use of the syllabary for writing Cherokee; they set up a national capital; elected a national body of legislators; published a newspaper, the *Cherokee Phoenix* (New Echota, 1828–1835); took steps to eliminate the system of blood revenge that had been rife among them; and set up a judicial system and law-enforcement body. In the midst of this rapid development of an intense national consciousness, gold was discovered in northern Georgia.

As white settlers rushed to the goldfields, the state of Georgia began a systematic effort to get rid of the Cherokees and take over their land, which in 1785 had been guaranteed by federal treaty. Reaction to the removal policy caused the Cherokee Nation to split. One small faction under the leadership of The Ridge, a distinguished Cherokee who had earlier helped write a law calling for death to any Cherokee who signed away tribal land, urged acceptance of the removal policy. The great majority, under the leadership of John Ross (1790–1866), strongly opposed removal and began determined but unsuccessful efforts in Washington to maintain their land. When Congress approved a new treaty with the support of President Andrew Jackson, the Ross segment finally had to be forcibly removed by the army. The Trail of Tears, as the hardships of removal were recorded in their history, resulted in the death of some 4,000 Cherokees. The operation was not completed until 1839, when all except the Eastern Band were finally placed in Indian Territory. There the leaders of the party that had favored removal were promptly assassinated.

Once removal was accomplished, the Cherokees set themselves to build anew the sort of society they had established in Georgia, putting their constitution and national laws into effect, setting up a representative national council, passing legislation making the new land a collective holding for the benefit of all, and devoting special attention to organizing a public school system. By 1887, the Cherokees had excellent schools; they were largely literate in both Cherokee and English, had established a new newspaper the *Cherokee Advocate*, printed in both languages, and were on the way to political and economic development comparable to that of other Americans. They had weathered another split over the issue of supporting the Union in the Civil War, the majority seeking to remain neutral but ultimately yielding to pressures from the Confederacy.

Their uncompromising stand against allotting their land and giving up the surplus under the General Allotment Act of 1887 led to defeat. Not only was the land broken up into individual allotments against their protests, but also their reestablished government was dissolved. By 1907 the Cherokees no longer existed as a distinct political entity in the United States. They did exist, however, as a distinct people, as was demonstrated in many activities through the 20th century. New religious integration based on reinvigorating traditional tribal concepts was manifested in the Redbird Smith movement. In 1944 Cherokees played a major role in organizing and leading the National Congress of American Indians. The Cherokee language continues to be spoken and the writing of it encouraged, and during the 1960s there was a burst of interest in the study and interpretation of Cherokee history.

Choctaws

The Choctaws are the third largest of the Five Civilized Tribes, with a population in Oklahoma estimated in the 1960s between 20,000 and 40,000. There are also communities in Mississippi and Louisiana with a total population of about 3,000, some of whom are descendants of Choctaws who escaped removal. The only reservation is in Mississippi.

The approximately 30,000 in Oklahoma are concentrated in 13 counties in the southeastern part of the state, where the Choctaw Nation was once located. In the 1970s there were many small communities of full-blood people devoted to the rural way of life that characterized most Choctaws for nearly 200 years, culturally a combination of southern Anglo-American and native customs and techniques. However, Choctaws, like the Cherokees, are also widely dispersed in cities throughout Oklahoma and elsewhere and vary considerably in occupation and income. Like the Cherokees, they are chiefly Baptists, Methodists, and Presbyterians, but some also participate in native forms of religious life in the "stomp grounds" and other ceremonial centers, probably to a lesser extent than Cherokees and Creeks. The Choctaw language is the language of the home in 30 percent or more of the rural families. They gave the state its name, *okla* meaning "people" and *homa*, "red" in their language.

The Choctaws' political organization consists of a principal chief appointed by the president of the United States and an advisory council elected annually by popular vote. This organization defends Choctaw interests before the Indian Claims Commission and, through a business committee, handles tribal affairs, such as maintaining a tribal roll based on the 1907 roll for the distribution of per capita payments resulting from claims cases.

The Choctaws, a Muskogean-speaking group, originally lived in the central portion of what became Mississippi and western Alabama. In this area is the sacred center of their country, preserved as a prehistoric mound site, called Nanih Waya. Like the other Civilized Tribes, the Choctaws were agricultural, village Indians; there were at least 115 villages or towns in the Mississippi area in the 18th century. They allied themselves with the French after 1699, a move that brought them into wars against the Chickasaws and the Natchez. During the early 1800s the Choctaws, under the leadership of able men such as Pushmataha, Apukshunnubbee, and Moshulatubbee, became steadily more committed to cooperation with the Americans and little inclined to support either military opposition, as urged by Tecumseh, or vigorous legal opposition, as pursued by the Cherokees. They were inclined to follow the ways of whites and allowed missionaries to establish schools. Many of them learned to use English, but they also developed a written form of Choctaw. In the late 19th century, converts to Methodism became influential in tribal affairs, and a systematic effort was begun to alter their governmental system along American lines. A national council of elected representatives from each of the traditional four districts was created, but the hereditary chieftainship through clan membership, instead of being abolished, was combined with new forms of representation. Before 1830 a code of laws was developed, alcohol was prohibited (although the ban was not well enforced), trials for persons accused of witchcraft were instituted, and a police force of "light horsemen" was created.

In 1820, as the desire of whites for the good cotton land in Alabama and Mississippi intensified, the Choctaws began to sign treaties ceding parts of their territory in return for land west of the Mississippi. In 1830 they signed the Treaty of Dancing Rabbit Creek, an agreement of vital importance in Choctaw history. It provided for a perpetual grant by the U.S. government of the southern half of Indian Territory if the Choctaws ceded their Mississippi lands. The government promised the usual annual payments, in this case $6,000 a year, in return for some 6 million acres. In the same year Mississippi passed laws giving Choctaws citizenship if they would relinquish tribally held land and accept individual allotments. A few did so, but 20,000 agreed to move to Indian Territory. Removal took place over three years, and a cholera epidemic and inadequate food and shelter en route took 5,000 lives. In 1833 the Choctaws became the first of the eastern tribes to settle in Indian Territory.

Establishing themselves as the Choctaw Nation on their 3 million acres, they proceeded to make a rapid new adaptation. The wealthiest Choctaws of Mississippi had brought their slaves with them, some families with as many as 500. They immediately began breaking and cultivating the new land and were soon raising cotton, corn, pecans, hogs, and cattle. They developed transportation systems both across country and along the navigable Arkansas River. A vigorous reaction against changing to new ways, headed by the able hereditary chief Moshulatubbee in the northern district was short-lived. In 1842 a school system was established, consisting of neighborhood day schools and boarding schools and was vigorously developed for the next 50 years; in 1853 a superintendent of public instruction for the whole nation was chosen. The Choctaws revamped their governmental system slowly and experimentally, in contrast with the Cherokees. By 1860 a constitution was accepted, and an elected principal chief, bicameral legislature and a court system were established. The Choctaws maintained great political solidarity; not even the Civil War split them. They allied themselves with the Confederacy but maintained an independent political position. Later, in a statesmanlike paper, their leaders pointed out that their support of the Confederacy had seemed the best way at the time to preserve their own distinct nationality. They made a separate peace with the Union. Deliberations of the council were always in the Choctaw language, although laws and actions were also translated into English. Choctaw names ceased to be used after the 1850s; families prominent in politics were the McCurtains, the Wrights, and the Joneses.

Pressures mounted in Indian Territory during the 1880s for the elimination of the Choctaw (and other Indian) governments and the breakup of the collectively held land into individual holdings. As with all the Civilized Tribes, factions arose as a result of these pressures, and although some violence did occur, the differences were eventually healed by political means. Ultimately, however, they were forced to yield to the implacable U.S. Congress. The Choctaw government was dissolved during the first decade of the 20th century, the land was divided, and the surplus sold. Choctaws, who had always segregated Negroes in schools and excluded them from voting or holding office in the Choctaw Nation, fought bitterly over whether Negroes should have equal assignment of allotments. Unlike the Chickasaws, they finally allowed equal division with Negro members of their nation.

Creeks

Although the BIA agency in Okmulgee, Okla., listed only about 10,000 Creeks, conservative estimates of the number eligible for claims payments reached 45,000 in 1970. The

Creeks therefore can probably be rated as the second largest of the Five Civilized Tribes.

They are concentrated in seven counties of east-central Oklahoma, north of the Choctaws and southwest of the Cherokees. The full-bloods in the tribe vigorously maintain native religious ways and customs, but they also send their children to public schools and belong to the Methodist, Baptist, or Presbyterian churches. Since the formal dissolution of their national government in 1906, they have used the designation Creek Tribe of Oklahoma and have maintained a tribal organization consisting of a general council of elected representatives from each of what had been the tribe's basic political units for more than a hundred years; called towns, the modern settlements are based on the traditional Creek towns, which were composed of several villages. The council also includes members elected by Seminoles living west of the Creek region. The representatives meet regularly at their Oklahoma capital, Okmulgee, to deal with matters of education and welfare, chiefly through the Bureau of Indian Affairs. There is also an elected business committee and three credit associations, also organized on the town basis. There is, in addition, the nominal office of principal chief, appointed by the president of the United States.

Many of the Creek towns maintain another ancient institution, namely, the "square grounds" or "stomp grounds," where regular meetings are devoted to traditional dances, rites connected with the sacred fire, and annual ceremonies such as the Green Corn rites. The traditional ball games are also sometimes played.

The mixed-bloods, including many persons whose ancestry is white, black, and Indian, live in cities and towns of eastern Oklahoma, particularly Tulsa, Eufaula, and others in the territory of the old Creek Nation. They work in a wide range of occupations, whereas the majority of full-bloods are farmers living in the heart of the Upper Creek area of the old Creek Nation.

The Creeks, who lived in northern Georgia and a large part of Alabama along the Alabama, Chattahoochee, and Flint rivers, played a major role in the development of trade after the arrival of Europeans in the southeastern states. They spoke a Muskogean language and called themselves Maskoke. During the 17th and 18th centuries they formed what the whites called a confederacy, a loose organization of friendly and allied tribes, including the Alabamas, Apalachees, Hitchitis, Yuchis, Natchez, and a band of the Shawnees, for the purpose of maintaining peace. The confederacy was also notable for its absorption of lesser groups. Generally they conceived of themselves as having two major divisions, the Upper Creeks, with a principal town at Tukabatchee in eastern Alabama, and the Lower Creeks, with a major town at Coweta in northern Georgia. The Coweta Creeks, generally accepted as the dominant segment during the early 18th century, maintained an alliance with the British and against the Spaniards, although they favored a policy of neutrality concerning the Europeans and their struggles for power.

For about twenty years after the Revolution a prominent Upper Creek named Alexander McGillivray (c. 1759–1793) worked to unify the Creeks and align them with the United States. The unity he achieved was broken during the first quarter of the 19th century, the period of influence of William McIntosh (c. 1775–1825), a Lower Creek. One source of cleavage was the cession of lands to the United States, which went on constantly through lesser *mikos* (headmen), so that by 1811 the general Creek council imposed the death sentence on any Creek who signed land cession treaties with the Americans.

In 1811 and 1812 Tecumseh made a great effort to enlist the Creeks, as well as other southern Indians, in his pan-Indian resistance movement. This split the Creeks; most opposed him, under the leadership of Pushmataha, but one group called the Red Sticks favored his plans and during 1814 fought against the Americans and against the Creeks who opposed them. American troops under Andrew Jackson not only defeated the fighting Creeks but also forced them to conclude treaty ceding most of their land in Georgia, including that of the loyal majority. More land cessions were made in 1825, but the treaty was annulled. A new treaty in 1826 ceded most Creek land east of the Mississippi to the Americans and contained an agreement that all Creeks would move to Indian Territory.

Some Creeks were given the privilege of accepting land allotments in Mississippi and thereby becoming American citizens. Others, chiefly followers of William McIntosh, who had been executed for selling land, went to Indian Territory in 1828, where they were opposed by Osages and Delawares, who regarded them as encroaching on their lands. In 1832 a final treaty left the remaining Creeks with no land east of the Mississippi. In-fighting developed, and although a few Creeks joined the Seminoles in Florida who were fighting against removal, most refused to move. In 1836 General Winfield Scott was ordered to lead the forced migration, despite Creek opposition. Of the more than 17,000 Creeks who started the two-year trek on the Trail of Tears, only 15,000 safely arrived in Indian Territory. Within months after arrival 3,500 more died of disease or starvation.

Once in Indian Territory in 1839, the Creeks worked for unity, at first accepting the leadership of the McIntosh faction. They established an organization along the lines of their old confederacy, which was strongly democratic. The old town structure was at its base, with each town having a principal chief and an elected council. Their written code of laws was expanded and approved in 1840 by the whole council of what was called the Creek Nation. There was still a division between Lower Creeks, who tended to be receptive to newer ways, and Upper Creeks, who tended to be strongly conservative; the latter dominated, but differences were settled in council meetings rather than by violence.

The national council prohibited missionaries from preaching, but, like the Cherokees, did allow them to establish schools. Baptists, Presbyterians, and Methodists created neighborhood and boarding schools, which many Creeks attended. The national council also continued its traditional policy of welcoming other Indian peoples like the Delawares, Shawnees, Kickapoos, Quapaws, and Miamis, as well as the Seminoles, but only after the U.S. government purchased some Creek land on which to establish them. They were active in encouraging intertribal organization and cooperation among the tribes of Indian Territory. The Creeks were split by the Civil War, but in 1867 promulgated another constitution that helped reunite them. In this reorganization they designated Okmulgee as their capital and established a bicameral body composed of a House of Kings and a House of Warriors, based on the old traditions, which functioned effectively as an elected body.

The old conflicts, as well as some new ones, resulted in the Green Peach War of 1881, as a host of outside pressures for railroad rights of way and other land encroachments came to a head. The factions were led by Isparharcher, a full-blood who had favored the North, and Checote, a Confederate sympathizer. The new divisions were quieted by this outbreak, and the full-bloods reasserted dominance under Isparharcher as principal chief. He and most of the Creeks were adamant against accepting land allotment, with the inevitable result—the dissolution of the Creek government in 1906 under the Curtis Act. A later nativistic movement led by Chitto Harjo failed to obtain general Creek support for reestablishing the old laws, but the tradition of the sacred fire and other religious rites continue to be the basis for the traditional square-grounds ceremonial activities.

Chickasaws

By the 1970s there were more Chickasaws in Oklahoma than had ever been reported in the course of their history; estimates ran from 5,500 to 9,000, the differing figures resulting from the same factors as in the case of the other Five Civilized Tribes—that is, varying degrees of cultural assimilation and wide dispersal of the population. The Chickasaws, more than the other five peoples, had lost their full-blood conservative segment by the 1970s. The mixed-bloods are in the great majority and have been for several generations.

Chickasaws are prominent in the professions, as cattlemen, and in various other occupations. They are scattered through Oklahoma but are to some extent concentrated in several south-central counties, where they were assigned land in the 1830s and 1840s. The majority are Methodists, and some are Baptists. There are no organized forms of native religion. They maintain a political organization consisting of a federally appointed governor, an elected tribal council, and the Chickasaw Tribal Protective Association. These organizations deal with claims cases and other business matters and ceremonial-symbolic functions. The Chickasaws show considerable interest in maintaining a symbol of their nationhood through the annual election of a tribal princess, who appears in the American Indian Exposition at Anadarko.

At the time of Hernando de Soto's expedition in the 1540s into what are now the southeastern states, there were approximately 4,000 Chickasaws, who occupied the area of northwestern Alabama, northern Mississippi, western Tennessee and Kentucky, with a corridor to the hunting grounds of the Ohio Valley. During the colonial period they were concentrated in large villages in northern Mississippi along the Tombigbee River. They were strongly agricultural. Their overall tribal organization was headed by a man the whites called a king, whose office was hereditary, and who was advised by a council. They exhibited a capacity for military effectiveness and strongly resisted domination by any other people: they defeated de Soto in 1541 when he ordered them to supply him with carriers, they remained independent of French domination—even absorbing remnants of the Natchez tribe after their devastating defeat by the French

—and they resisted domination by the Creeks who invaded their territory in 1795.

During the 18th century they became well known as traders; after 1763 the Chickasaws tended to ally themselves with the British in the three-way European power struggle for control of American territory. Until late in the American Revolution they favored the British, but a pro-American faction grew among them and by 1786, when the Hopewell Treaty was signed with other tribes, they were cooperating with the new government. Between 1800 and 1818 they made treaties with the Americans, ceding large portions of their territory, and in 1813–1814 they fought the Creek Red Sticks on the side of the Americans.

A small mixed-blood group dominated their internal politics, using the traditional king and council form of government to rule the trading empire they controlled. By 1829 they had formulated a body of laws. During the 1830s they negotiated but did not resist strongly the removal pressures that were impinging on all the Civilized Tribes, in which they were included because of the extent to which they had adopted European-derived ways. They signed a treaty in 1833 agreeing to move to Indian Territory, to pay the Choctaws $53,000 for rights as citizens in the Choctaw Nation in Indian Territory, and to sell their 6 million acres of land in Mississippi.

Their removal took place over 13 years, not being completed until 1850. Like the others who traveled the Trail of Tears, they suffered many hardships and perhaps 1,000 died en route. Until 1854 the Chickasaws did little to reestablish their tribe as it had been in Mississippi. Instead they were content to live on the annuities they received for their eastern lands and to drift within the new location as citizens of the Choctaw Nation. Gradually, however, their spirit returned. In 1855 they made an agreement to separate from the Choctaws, whom they accused (probably unjustly) of tyrannical controls over them. They moved to the lands they had originally paid the Choctaws for, along the Canadian River, and reorganized their political and economic life. They wrote a constitution; set up an elected governor, a legislative body composed of a senate and house of representatives, and a court system; elected a superintendent of public instruction; and began to build a school system comparable to that of the other Civilized Tribes. The Civil War, which they entered on the side of the Confederacy, interrupted their political and educational development. When it resumed, the invasion of settlers into Indian Territory profoundly interfered with their progress.

Pressures began for the formation, bitterly opposed by the Chickasaws, of a territorial government that would supersede the Indian national governments. When the General Allotment Act was passed in 1887, it became clear that the whites were determined to break up the Indians' collective land holdings and, if necessary, the local governments that the Chickasaws and the other peoples had built; in 1893 the allotment policy began to be applied to the Five Civilized Tribes. To overcome Chickasaw opposition, the Curtis Act was passed in 1898, dissolving the Chickasaw government and instituting individual allotment. From that time their cultural assimilation proceeded more rapidly than among the other Civilized Tribes.

Comanches and Kiowas

In the 1960s there were about 2,700 Comanches and the same number of Kiowas, as well as some 400 Kiowa-Apaches, in Oklahoma. They live in southwestern Oklahoma on individually owned tracts of land; four tracts of collectively owned land are held in trust by the U.S. government. Some whites are interspersed among them on this land, which was bought from the U.S. government or from Indians to whom it had been allotted. A BIA agency at Anadarko provides some federal services and attends to property trust matters. The population of the Comanches is about what it was during initial contact with whites in the southern plains country; the Kiowas' population is probably 1,000 greater than it was.

Comanches, Kiowas, and Kiowa-Apaches are organized as a business corporation through the Kiowa-Comanche-Apache Business Committee, on which Comanches and Kiowas are equally represented, with members elected for four-year terms. The purpose of the committee is to take care of various tribal interests in accord with the Oklahoma Indian Welfare Act of 1936 and in conjunction with the BIA agency. The Indians live on scattered homesteads as farmers or stock raisers, but many have moved to cities in other states or to the larger cities in Oklahoma. Methodists and Dutch Reformed church members predominate among the Comanches, while Kiowas belong to the Catholic, Methodist, Episcopal, and Baptist churches. A considerable number in each group are members of the Native American church, and some profess the native tribal religions. All participate actively in the annual American Indian Exposition at Anadarko, one of the most heavily attended and best-known expressions of pan-Indian ceremonialism and pageantry in the United States. Kiowas especially have become well known for artistic endeavors, particularly painting, which has been encouraged by the University of Oklahoma since 1927. The writer N. Scott Momaday, a Kiowa and professor of English literature at Stanford University, won the Pulitzer prize in 1969 for the novel *House Made of Dawn.*

The Comanche and Kiowa languages belong to different linguistic stocks—Comanche being Uto-Aztecan and Kiowa being Tanoan—but the two tribes have been closely associated for more than 100 years, and their recent histories are similar. They both lived originally in the eastern Rocky Mountains, the Comanches probably in the Wyoming area and the Kiowas in Montana. Both moved eastward beginning in the late 1600s, the Comanches into the country of the North Platte River in Nebraska and the Kiowas into South Dakota. In these new locations they acquired horses and became more nomadic and warlike. The Sioux and the Cheyennes pushed them south, and they in turn fought with the Eastern Apaches and the New Mexico Spaniards. In these raids the Comanches, especially, took many Spanish prisoners and became mixed genetically with them as well as with other Indian foes. Both tribes were established by the late 1700s in what became western Kansas, Oklahoma, and eastern Texas, the Kiowas along the Arkansas River and its tributaries, the Comanches along the Canadian River. From these locations in the southern buffalo country, they raided New Mexico, Texas, and as far south as Chihuahua, Mexico. Their adaptation to the horse and buffalo culture was as thoroughgoing as that of any Plains Indians, and for nearly 100 years they were the terror of the Spaniards and later the Mexicans and Texans. The Texans were so fearful of their raiding that they estimated the Comanche population at 20,000 when there were barely more than 2,000.

In 1790, after many years of mutual raiding, the Kiowas and the Comanches made peace with each other, but they remained at war with the Cheyennes and Osages for another 50 years. As Americans came into their territory, hostilities developed. Numerous efforts were made by the Americans to make peace treaties, but these failed, especially after Texans in 1840 murdered a group of ten Comanche headmen who had come to a peace conference. Americans moving west were constantly infiltrating the territory of the two tribes. In 1853 a coalition of resisting tribes, consisting of Comanches, Kiowas, Cheyennes, Osages, Arapahos, and others attempted to wipe out the encroaching whites once and for all but were defeated by an alliance of Sauks and Foxes and other settled Indians fighting for the whites in Indian Territory.

From this time the whites redoubled their treaty-making efforts, but they had little success until the Treaty of Medicine Lodge in 1867. The Comanches and Kiowas were to settle on 3 million acres in southwestern Indian Territory, which the government had forced the Choctaws and Chickasaws to cede. A small minority of both groups went to live there and to receive the meager rations promised in the treaty. About 1,000 Comanches and fewer Kiowas lived on the new reservation, a tiny portion of the land over which they had formerly ranged.

Most of the Indians still lived in their old territory and continued, along with the reservation residents, to raid into Texas and Mexico. The federal government, after unsuccessfully trying President Ulysses S. Grant's peace policy, brought in more troops. In the resulting clashes 26 Kiowa leaders, including their most respected men, were sent to Florida for imprisonment, where several died. At the same time the Comanches moved in a different direction. During 1873–1874 a messiah named Ishatai persuaded the young warriors that they could wipe out the whites and bring back the buffalo. The first uprising stimulated by the preacher ended in miserable defeat, and his influence waned.

During the 1880s the last holdout bands came onto the reservation, including one headed by the distinguished Comanche, Quanah, who became known as Quanah Parker. By then 50 percent of the people were living on rations and did so until 1901. During the 1890s the Comanches and Kiowas began to farm and raise cattle, but to a large extent they lived by leasing grazing rights to whites, who were pushing hard on all sides for land. During the 1880s the Comanches through their Mexican contacts played an important role in spreading the Native American church, which Quanah Parker helped found.

Pawnees

From a population of 10,000 in the 1830s, the Pawnees were reduced to about 700 in 1900 and seemed destined for extinction. By the 1960s, however, their population had increased to a reported figure of about 1,200. The Pawnees live in Pawnee and Payne counties in north-central Oklahoma, at the southern edge of the earliest known range of one of their bands.

They live on individual allotments on some 28,000 acres, about one-tenth of what had been their federal reservation in 1892. They are for the most part small farmers and stock raisers on not very productive land, making as much of their living from leasing grazing- and farm-land to whites as from their own activities. They are organized as the Pawnee Indian Tribe of Oklahoma under a constitution and bylaws chartered by the state under the Indian Welfare Act of 1936. The tribal organization includes the four distinct bands that have always characterized the Pawnees. The band chiefs make up what is called the Nasharo Council, which meets regularly and contributes to the Pawnee sense of common identity. There is also a business council with eight elected members. Most Pawnees are at least nominally Methodists, some are members of the Native American church, and a large number participate to some degree in traditional religious ceremonials. They are active in the annual American Indian Convention at Anadarko and in pan-Indian activities around the United States.

The Pawnee language belongs to the Caddoan linguistic family, to which the Caddos and the Wichitas of Oklahoma also belong. Before the European invasions began, the Pawnees and linguistically related groups were probably concentrated chiefly in the lower Mississippi Valley. Their culture was based on intensive agriculture, and they lived in settled villages of closely clustered, elaborately built earth lodges. Their religion made use of sacred medicine bundles, visions, and organized ceremonial societies. The annual sacrifice of a young woman captive to the morning-star deity was an important ceremonial.

In 1720, when the Spaniards first made contact with them, the Skidi Band of the Pawnees was living in what became eastern Nebraska and Kansas. This band, which had become active buffalo hunters on foot, pioneered the westward movement of the Pawnees, stimulated first by their interest in buffalo hunting and later by pressure from eastern Indians who were displaced by the early white settlers. The Pawnees made increasing use of horses as they moved west and made contact with the developing nomad cultures of the plains—the Kiowas, Comanches, Arikaras, and Sioux.

By the end of the 17th century some Pawnees had already settled in what is now central Nebraska, and some eight villages on the Republican River reportedly had a population of more than 10,000 about 1700. Throughout the 1700s more Pawnees (such as the group called the Black Pawnees) moved west and were in touch with French traders prior to 1750. They never made war on the United States; on the contrary, they were allied with the Americans in their efforts to control the raiding of Sioux, Osages, and Comanches. In 1818 they made a treaty of peace with the U.S. government and then from 1833 through 1857 made treaties ceding all their territory except for a small reservation along the Loup River in east-central Nebraska. As they settled on this reservation, they engaged in warfare with the Sioux, allied with the U.S. cavalry as effective scouts.

All during the 19th century the Pawnees suffered a succession of devastating misfortunes. Shortly after 1800 a severe smallpox epidemic reduced their many villages to one. Smallpox continued to afflict them through the 1830s, with 5,000 reported dying during that decade. At the same time their numbers were further reduced in raids by the Sioux and other nomadic tribes contending for the buffalos. By 1893 there were only 821 Pawnees left. In that year, after acquiring a reservation in Oklahoma in return for giving up their land in Nebraska, they were immediately forced to break up the reservation into individual allotments, with the surplus land opened to settlement by whites. Rations were cut by the government in order to force more farming, but this had the reverse effect, leading the Pawnees to depend on lease money from white cattlemen and farmers.

In 1891–1892, as forced allotment became imminent, the

Pawnees actively adopted the Ghost Dance religion, but its leader was imprisoned and the movement forced underground. Whites then suggested that if allotments went through, the Pawnees would no longer be under federal government supervision and could freely practice the Ghost Dance. During these years the peyote cult spread among the Pawnees. The Ghost Dance died out, but the Native American church continued.

During the 20th century Pawnees increasingly adapted to Anglo-American ways. In 1962, in a suit against the federal government for illegally taken land, the Indian Claims Commission awarded the Pawnees $7 million, which was administered by their tribal organization to improve their economic condition.

Shawnees

In 1970 about 2,250 Shawnees lived in Oklahoma. The tribe is divided into three fairly distinct groups living in different parts of the state, with the largest number, some 1,100 individuals, living among Cherokees and whites in northeastern Oklahoma. A group of 450 living in the extreme northeastern corner of the state are known as the Eastern Shawnees; intermixed with Senecas and some other groups, their history has been rather separate from that of the other Shawnees for more than a century. In central Oklahoma near the town of Shawnee are another 700, who were long known as the Absentee Shawnees.

The Shawnees maintain two tribal organizations. Those in the vicinity of Shawnee are organized as the Absentee Shawnee Tribe of Indians of Oklahoma and have an elected council and principal chief. Those in the northeastern part of the state are organized as the Eastern Shawnee Tribe of Oklahoma in accord with the Oklahoma Indian Welfare Act of 1936. Both tribal organizations maintain business committees that handle land and other matters in conjunction with agencies of the Bureau of Indian Affairs.

Shawnees are farmers and stock raisers and work in a variety of occupations like those of the whites in the region. Some are Christian, belonging to congregations of Methodists, Baptists, or the Society of Friends, and a large percentage follow traditional religious ways. The Big Kim Band of the Absentee Shawnees is the most active community in the annual Thanksgiving and War ceremonials. Few know the Shawnee language, which belongs to the Algonkian linguistic family.

In the 1600s there may have been no more than 3,000 Shawnees, apparently living in the Ohio River Valley. Their known migrations began before 1690, when they were driven from their settlements by the west-ranging Iroquois. From that time until the 1870s they moved about more than any other Indian group except the Delawares and the Kickapoos. In their moves they separated into distinct groups that lived apart for many years at a time.

Most of the Shawnees first migrated southwest as far as South Carolina and Georgia, and one village became established among the Creeks in Alabama. Later they separated into two groups, one moving north to join the Delawares, with whom they had friendly relations, in the Susquehanna Valley in Pennsylvania, another group moving northwest into Tennessee along the Cumberland River. Others ranged into Florida in small units during the 1700s. The Tennessee group was then pushed northward by attacks from Cherokees and Chickasaws and by 1730 had moved as far north as Ohio. In 1755, as a result of the pressures of whites in Pennsylvania and of the Iroquois ordering the Delawares to leave eastern Pennsylvania, the Shawnees of the east also moved to Ohio, so that for a time they were joined again with the other bands of Shawnees. Despite this fragmentation, they maintained the Shawnee language, and many remained devoted to their religious traditions. They produced one of the ablest Indian leaders, who worked for unity among all the Indians east of the Mississippi—Tecumseh (c. 1768–1813). The Shawnees generally assisted the French against the

British in the struggle for control of the fur trade and the land west of the Appalachians. Their Ohio settlements were allied with other Algonkians who were opposing the westward advance of the English. Under these conditions a movement for Indian unity arose at the end of the 18th century. The political aim of this movement, for which Tecumseh was spokesman, was to prevent any further cessions of land to whites. Culturally, it was a nativistic religious movement spearheaded by the prophet Tenskwatawa, Tecumseh's brother, who preached rejection of white man's ways and a return to Indian customs. The religious movement took hold among the Algonkian peoples who had been displaced and those native to the Ohio-Indiana region. Tecumseh, noted as a war leader, made a great effort to bring the strong southeastern tribes such as the Creeks into his resistance movement, but failed. In 1811 the Prophet's Town in Indiana where Tenskwatawa's followers had settled in large numbers was destroyed by U.S. military action, and in 1813 Tecumseh was killed while fighting with the British against the Americans.

With the end of British support after the War of 1812, the embattled Algonkians began to give way, selling their lands in Ohio and Indiana and moving west in 1831 to a reservation in eastern Kansas, where they began to farm. Other Shawnees had moved to Missouri before 1800 and then southwest to Arkansas, Indian Territory, and to Texas on the Brazos River. Eventually, the Shawnees in Kansas were forced to give up their reservation and buy land in Oklahoma with the proceeds. Later all the Shawnees moved to their three present locations in Oklahoma. The Eastern Shawnees, mixed with Senecas, had settled in what became northeastern Oklahoma as early as 1832. The Shawnees who had moved before 1800 to Texas and were pushed out 50 years later were moved to central Oklahoma; they became the nucleus of the Absentee Shawnee community. Like many other Indian Territory peoples, their lands were allotted during the period 1891–1893, and they became individual property owners or promptly lost their land to whites.

Osages

The approximately 1,100 Osages living in Oklahoma in the 1920s were described by some as the wealthiest people in the world. Every individual in 1925 was receiving $13,200 a year as a headright to oil and gas lease proceeds. The headright is still the main source of income of those identifying themselves as Osages. From 1920 to about 1970 the group received some $500 million. Their income per person was reduced by the 1970s, but it was still substantial. One reason for reduction was that in 1970 nearly eight times as many people—8,244—were listed as Osages. The right to receive income from the Osage oilfield led many to identify as tribal members who were not interested earlier.

Although a majority of Osages still make their homes in Osage County, nearly as many live in southern California, and others are scattered through 36 different states in some 300 different U.S. communities. They work in a variety of occupations; among those who have distinguished themselves are the Tallchief sisters, Maria and Marjorie, both ballet dancers, and Major General Clarence L. Tinker (1887–1942).

The Osages in Oklahoma are still organized under the provisions of the special act of Congress of 1906, without constitution or corporate charter. A principal chief, assistant chief, and council of eight, elected every four years, are chiefly concerned with leasing the oilfield and using tribal funds. The tribe pays for the expenses of the BIA agency at Pawhuska and has established a health clinic and other services for Osages in Oklahoma. Osages are predominantly Catholic, but some are Baptist, Methodist, or members of the Society of Friends. In 1918 there were 25 congregations of the Native American church, but the participants declined in numbers through subsequent years. In some homes a Siouan language is still spoken.

Before the entry of the English into Virginia, the Osages lived in the Piedmont area and also along the Ohio River in what became Kentucky. By 1673 they had encountered Europeans along the Osage River in western Missouri. They were strongly agricultural but also hunted buffalo. They lived in circular skin-covered lodges or in tipis when hunting buffalo.

The Osages allied themselves with the French traders and military from about 1712, but by 1790 they had become opposed to the French and then to the Spanish. They remained largely independent of all alliances with other tribes or with Europeans and resisted various efforts of the Spaniards to control their trade with and military action against other Indians. They began ceding land to the United States in 1808 and by 1825 had been given a reservation in Kansas, which many refused to settle on for some time. In these decades there was fighting between Osages and Cherokees on land that the Osages claimed. By 1839 most of them had moved to the Kansas reservation, where they continued to hunt buffalo and to raid and be raided by Plains tribes.

During their residence in Kansas from 1839 until 1871, the Osages established military alliances with Comanches, Kiowas, and Apaches and prospered through trade. By 1847 the pressures of invading white settlers began. The government forced the Osages to cede part of the reservation, but that did not slow down the invaders. In 1868 they were forced to sell the rest of the reservation to a railroad company and to buy land in Indian Territory. By 1872, 4,000 Osages with 12,000 horses were settled south of Pawhuska. In 1881 they approved a constitution modeled on the Cherokees'; law and order were kept through a court and police system. By 1893 half of the reservation was leased to white farmers and cattlemen. Under the leadership of Bigheart, the Osages resisted allotment, and the process was suspended until 1906. When they were forced to accept allotment, they arranged to retain subsurface rights to minerals and oil in the name of the tribe and managed to have all land allotted to Osages, with no surplus for whites. Thus each Osage received 658 acres and a $3,819 share of the tribal fund. Eventually Osage County became a reservation—the only present-day reservation in Oklahoma—with the subsurface rights held as tribal trust.

Other Indians living in Oklahoma in the 1970s were the following: the Arapahos, Biloxis, Caddos, Cayugas, Southern Cheyennes, Iowas, Kaws, Miamis, Missouris, Modocs, Otoes, Ottawas, Peorias, Poncas, Quapaws, Senecas, Tonkawas, Wichitas, and Wyandots.

THE NORTHERN PLAINS

The upper Missouri Valley region, including the Yellowstone and North Platte drainages and the headwaters of the Snake, may be called the northern plains. A region of prairie and high plains, it includes the states of North and South Dakota, Montana, and Wyoming. Formerly this was the major part of the buffalo's habitat; now it is an area of ranching and dry farming. The northern plains contain some 16 distinct Indian groups, although these can be counted in several ways, so that if all the varieties of Sioux and others were listed separately, for example, the number could be as high as 29. The population of Indians in the whole region in 1960 was over 80,000, the bulk of whom lived on federal reservations, mostly small fractions of the lands claimed by the Indians before their first contacts with whites. Both the population and the number of Indian ethnic groups are about the same as they have been for the past 200 years. In fact, according to one estimate, the Indian population has increased by a few thousand since first contacts. Possibly four more groups identify separately from one another than was the case during the precontact period, resulting from place-

ment on separate reservations. The state most heavily populated by Indians was Montana, with some 40,000; South Dakota was close behind with 33,150; North Dakota had 5,800;
and Wyoming, about 3,300.

Some 250 years before the arrival of white settlers, Indian
groups moved freely through the northern plains. The area
was occupied by tribes moving west from the Great Lakes,
by others moving from the Southeast, and by tribes moving
east from the Rocky Mountains. Later movements were
stimulated by opportunities for a new kind of life using guns
and horses, as well as by the pressures generated by European settlement in the East. Some of the newcomers who
began to arrive about the end of the 17th century relied almost entirely on buffalo hunting, others made a dual adjustment by hunting buffalo part of the year and living the rest
of the year by farming. The eastern Sioux never wholly de-
serted their former forest-based life for the nomadism of
buffalo-hunting. Some purely farming groups lived along
the larger rivers in permanent, densely populated villages. A
number of such peoples, the Mandans and Pawnees especially, never turned to the nomadic life but continued to be
sedentary, with buffalo hunting as a secondary source of
subsistence.

A second characteristic of the newly mobile peoples of the
northern plains was that they became especially concerned
with and adept in warfare. The competition for hunting
grounds was intense as more and more Indians moved into
the region. Thus for survival they developed fighting techniques, and warfare became a major orientation of their cultures.

It is important to note that the Indians of this region have
been characterized by their vigorous maintenance of cultural
values and identity; despite extremely adverse circumstances they have not only maintained their groups without
exception, but have also exerted a profound and continuing
cultural influence on nearly all the other tribes of the United
States. Their way of life also became the stereotype of the In-

dian way for whites, so they have played a special role in white history and culture as well.

Sioux

It does some violence to the realities of Sioux life to describe them as a whole, for there were in the 1960s at least ten distinct subgroups among the Sioux, the largest single group among the northern plains peoples. These groups all speak languages belonging to the Dakota family of the Siouan language stock. Their sense of identity as separate bands has to some extent been brought about or intensified by their placement on 13 different reservations.

In South Dakota in 1960 between 33,000 and 35,000 Siouan- or Dakota-speaking peoples lived on seven reservations under federal supervision. The largest of these reservations, on which the greatest number of Sioux are concentrated, are in southwestern South Dakota—the Pine Ridge and Rosebud reservations, the first with a population of 10,648, and the second with 8,183. The population of the other five reservations ranged from 4,307 to 705. In addition 289 Sioux live in a group of independent communities that do not constitute a reservation. In North Dakota there are two Sioux reservations with a population of 5,800. There are smaller reservations of Sioux in Montana, Minnesota, and Nebraska.

Nearly all of the Sioux of South and North Dakota live according to what seems superficially to be the white man's way; they live in frame houses like other rural Dakotans or in the dilapidated remains of log cabins that were built when they first relocated on the reservations. Nowhere do the traditional tipis appear as regular living quarters, although they are in evidence during summer ceremonials and in connection with other religious rites, such as the Peyote cult. About one-fifth raise cattle, and a much smaller number dry farm some land. The majority, some 60 percent, work for wages in nearby towns, for neighboring white farmers and Sioux stock raisers, or in BIA operations. The land on most reservations is checkerboarded, that is, partly occupied by whites who bought allotments from Indians or homesteaded the land when it was open for settlement after allotment. Thus Indians and whites are interspersed, and there is much mutual hostility.

As many as half the people on most reservations claim unmixed descent, but among the Sioux there is a well-recognized distinction between mixed-bloods and full-bloods, with mixed-bloods outnumbering full-bloods. As among the Cherokees, the distinction is primarily a matter of cultural differences. The term mixed-blood refers in ordinary usage to persons who follow the ways of non-Indians, speak English at home, strive to amass property, furnish their houses in white style, and either actively reject Sioux religious ways and values or rarely if ever participate in them. However, they do identify themselves as Indians, although full-bloods may regard them as less Sioux than themselves. Full-bloods speak one of the Dakota languages and encourage their children to do so, respect elements of traditional Sioux religion, participate in some of the surviving dances and other rituals, and in other ways pursue an Indian lifestyle. The distinction is obviously not a hard and fast one dividing the Sioux of any reservation community into sharply bounded segments, but it is a strong and important distinction in their thinking. Full-blood and mixed-blood are more fluid categories than the general distinction between Indians and whites.

Nearly all Dakotas are nominally members of Christian congregations—usually Episcopalian, Roman Catholic, Church of God, or an evangelical sect, and most participate to some degree in the organization and services of these churches. At the same time the Native American church has many practicing members, as does the Yuwipi cult, which is the chief surviving active tradition of the native Dakota religion. The two types of religion, Christian and traditional, are not regarded as mutually exclusive, although there is a strong tendency for members of the Native American church to ignore their Christian affiliations. The pow-wow gatherings, which stress traditional Dakota music and dance and portions of some ceremonials, are important in the lives of nearly all Dakotas on the reservations, and they present opportunities to maintain contacts with other Indians across the United States.

On most of the federal reservations tribal councils are organized under the provisions of the Indian Reorganization Act of 1934. These political bodies assume various functions related to the provision by the BIA of school, economic, law and order, and welfare services. These councils are the focus of active political interest and give rise to strong factional divisions, despite the fact that their political power is limited by the BIA supervisory role. There are also tribal courts with elected judges, which decide domestic and other cases. Most groups of Dakotas take an active part in the affairs of the National Congress of American Indians, and some are members of the militant American Indian Movement (AIM).

In 1973 the Dakotas won national attention when leaders of AIM occupied the town of Wounded Knee, S. Dak., the name of which gave prominence (as the leaders of AIM wished it to do) to one of the important symbols of Dakota collective identity. Indeed, many of the most important symbols of the troubled relations between whites and Indians—Sitting Bull, Red Cloud, the Ghost Dance, Wounded Knee, General Custer—derive from events in Sioux history of the late 19th century.

About 1680 all of the Dakota-speaking peoples, consisting of three major divisons—the Santees, the Wichiyelas (sometimes called Yankton), and the Tetons—were living around the headwaters of the Mississippi River in the Mille Lacs area of Minnesota. They were under pressure from the Chippewas moving west from the central Great Lakes, who had acquired guns from the French and other Europeans. As the Chippewas sought control of the hunting areas of the upper Mississippi, the Dakotas steadily moved westward, the Teton division moving first and prevailing against more westerly Indians, such as the Cheyennes and the Kiowas, in what became western South and North Dakota. In doing this the Tetons gave up entirely their forest way of life. They were followed by the Wichiyelas, who established themselves to the east and south and became primarily hunters. The Santees remained at the eastern edge of the prairie country bordering on the forest lands and maintained a mixed way of subsistence. As the Dakotas established themselves in new areas (the Tetons and Wichiyelas completely revolutionizing their way of life), they became the dominant peoples of the northern plains and the most thoroughly adapted as horse-riding buffalo hunters.

The Teton and Wichiyela Dakotas were at the height of their prosperity and military power during the first half of the 19th century. It was they who offered the most formidable resistance to the thousands of white immigrants who began to move across the plains after 1849. Their raids, along with those of the Cheyennes and Arapahos, in 1849 and 1850 led to strong efforts by the U.S. government to keep the wagon trains moving freely westward. In treaties, such as the Fort Laramie Treaty of 1851, the Indians agreed not to molest the settlers, in return for annuities and guarantees of peace. But the treaties were ineffective, and hostilities became more intense. Neither the Dakotas nor the U.S. cavalry were disciplined to follow the agreements, and conflicts continued.

Sitting Bull (c. 1834–1890), Red Cloud (1822–1909), and Crazy Horse (c. 1877) were formidable figures who attracted national attention. Red Cloud became a familiar figure to the U.S. officers, signing treaties, accepting their invitations to travel to Washington, making a speech at Cooperstown, N.Y., that caught the attention of the whole country, and moving back and forth between hostile and peaceful stances. The implacable Crazy Horse was a great war chief and a leader in the victory of the Sioux over Custer at the Little Bighorn in 1876. The superior weapons of the U.S. Army and their mobility, because of the newly built railroad, proved decisive in the long run. What had been set aside in 1868 as the Great Sioux Reservation (comprising most of what became North and South Dakota) was broken up, and the Dakotas began to settle into new, small reservations scattered across the northern plains. Red Cloud had to make peace, and the Dakotas were forced to accept the supervision of the BIA on nine reservations. The BIA prohibited the Sun Dance, the major expression of Dakota religious and community life, and the forced scattering of Indians into very small settlements or isolated homesteads began. The buffalo was soon wiped out by white hunters, and the Dakotas became dependent on government rations. American-style schools and churches were established, and by 1889 the authority of the chiefs was being undermined in a variety of ways by the Indian agents.

The Dakotas turned in 1889 to a new religion, the Ghost Dance, which originated among the Paiutes farther west. At Pine Ridge Reservation, when the Oglalas (a division of the Sioux) began enthusiastic dancing, the BIA representative and the cavalry officers misunderstood the nature of the new religious expression, regarding the rites as a signal for attacks on the whites. The result was the massacre of 128 Dakotas at Wounded Knee Creek. The event became known across the United States and symbolized what many whites had come to regard as the tragedy of the Indians and the injustice and incompetence of the government in dealing with them. Wounded Knee underlined the message of an influential book published a few years before, Helen Hunt Jackson's *A Century of Dishonor* (1881), an eloquent denunciation of injustices done to the Indians.

The government had begun to issue cattle to the Dakotas in 1885, and slowly they turned to cattle raising, with some success. By 1912, on the Pine Ridge Reservation alone, there were 40,000 head of cattle, and the situation was similar on other Sioux reservations. When World War I brought high prices for cattle, they sold nearly all their stock and leased their land to whites, who offered to pay high rents because of the chance to make great profits during the war boom. By 1918, as a result of the sale of cattle and the allotment and subsequent sale of land, most Dakotas on the reservations were living in poverty, which was aggravated when the Depression wiped out the leaseholders. By 1939 most of the employed Dakotas were working for wages or had moved away from the reservations to larger cities throughout the United States. The federal government made efforts during the 1940s to help reestablish the cattle industry, but by the 1960s not more than 7 or 8 percent of Dakotas were cattle owners, and the majority of these were barely making a living. Their depressed economic condition continued into the 1970s.

Crows

The Crows, whose name for themselves is Absaroka, have occupied a federal reservation in southern Montana since about 1868. They are the westernmost of the Siouan-speakers. In 1970, 4,992 Crows were listed as residents of the reservation, although 1,242 of these were not actually living there. The Crows hold 50 percent of the reservation in private ownership, as a result of allotment about 1900, but they lease most of this land to non-Indians. About 25 percent of the land is owned by whites, and another 13 percent is held in common title by the Crow tribe. Most resident Crows raise cattle on their own land or work for wages in BIA or tribal operations; 40 percent live largely by leasing their land to whites. The Crows maintained their aboriginal tribal organization after taking up residence on the reservation but reorganized in 1935 under the IRA. Their tribal council is unusually strong and independent. The majority of Crows are nominal Christians but are also active in the Native American church and regularly hold Sun Dance gatherings.

Like the Dakotas, the Crows completely adapted to the horse-riding, buffalo-hunting way of life, although it is likely that they were sedentary village-dwelling people before horses were introduced about 1740. They became active traders in the late 1700s, trading guns for horses with the Shoshones to their southwest. During the first half of the 19th century they developed the highly organized buffalo-hunting culture characteristic of the Dakotas and other northern Plains tribes. They fought other Indians to retain their territory east of the Rocky Mountains, and they claimed land as far east as the Black Hills. Their Plains culture traits included the vision quest for guardian spirits, the Sun Dance, and the war complex, including the counting of coups and the eagle-feather war bonnet. In contrast with the Dakotas, they were organized into clans with descent through the female line. In addition to men's age-graded societies there was the Tobacco Society, which treated tobacco as a sacred plant and managed ceremonies honoring the morning star.

Like other Plains tribes, the Crows suffered great population losses as a result of smallpox and cholera epidemics during the first half of the 19th century. From 4,000 to 5,000 when first recorded about 1780, their population declined by nearly half. By the 1960s their numbers had climbed again to about 5,000.

The experience of the Crows on the reservation has been much like that of the Dakotas, but they are less disorganized and their political organization is stronger. Like the Dakotas, they are active in intertribal pow-wows in which their costumes, ceremonials, dances, and music are influential.

Other Northern Plains Peoples

Before the invasion of the northern plains area by the Dakota-speaking peoples, Siouan tribes lived along several of the rivers, including the upper Missouri, as sedentary agricultural villagers. Notable among these were the Mandans, who lived in what became North and South Dakota. Together with a similar group of farmers, the Hidatsas, their population numbered more than 6,000. Their villages were composed of large earth lodges, built closely together in communities of as many as 1,000 to 1,500 people. Their complex culture resembled somewhat that of the Arikaras and Pawnees farther south, the Caddoan-speaking sedentary people of the southern plains. The Mandans lost population on a large scale during the epidemics of the early 1800s and were reduced to a handful of people. The Hidatsas were somewhat less hard hit. The remnant of the Mandans merged with the Hidatsas, and the resulting mixed small groups in the 1960s were living with the Gros Ventres, an Algonkian-speaking group formerly closely associated with the Arapaho, on the Fort Berthold Reservation in northwestern North Dakota.

The Assiniboines, reputed to have branched off from the Yankton Dakotas at about the time they moved west onto the plains, lived farther north in Canada, but portions of the tribe moved south in the 1860s and agreed to live on the Fort Peck and Fort Belknap reservations in northern Montana.

Blackfeet, Cheyennes, and Arapaho

In 1960 there were about 5,000 Blackfeet living on a reservation in northwestern Montana. Greatly reduced after a century of smallpox and cholera epidemics from 1781 on, the Blackfeet may have numbered as many as 15,000 in 1780, when whites first recorded their population. In 1960 about 2,000 Cheyennes lived on a reservation adjoining that of the Crows in southern Montana, and about 1,100 northern Arapaho, sometimes called Gros Ventres, lived on the the Fort Berthold Reservation in North Dakota.

The history of these Algonkian-speaking peoples is generally similar to that of the dominant Siouan-speaking groups of the region. There is no indication that the Blackfeet moved into the plains from the east, but the Cheyennes were first encountered by Europeans in western Minnesota, where they lived as sedentary farming people until the early 1800s. They obtained horses by the last quarter of the 18th century but did not start hunting buffalo on horseback until the 1840s. Along with the Crows, they engaged in frequent intertribal warfare, suffered well-known massacres at the hands of U.S. Cavalry at Sand Creek and Ash Hollow in Colorado, and participated with the Sioux in the defeat of Custer. Finally, in 1877–1878 they suffered defeats and were sent south to Oklahoma. Even though guarded by cavalry, they refused to remain in the state and marched north to their Wyoming-Montana homeland. They were forced again to the south, and when they resisted many were killed. In the 1880s they were reestablished beside the Crow Reservation in Montana, where they now live.

The Cheyenne, Blackfeet, and Arapaho experience on the reservations in Montana is similar to that of the other northern plains tribes—rations, slow adaptation to cattle raising, forced assimilation through schools, and regulations against their native religious practices. After the change in U.S. policy in the 1930s, they organized a tribal council under the IRA, revived the annual Sun Dance, and became vigorous participants in the peyote rites of the Native American church.

Other Indians living in the northern plains in the 1970s were the Arikaras, Atsinas, Chippewas, Crees, and Kutenais.

THE WESTERN BORDER OF THE PLAINS

Living in the eastern Rocky Mountains and their margins in the plains and also in the Great Basin are Indians who speak five distinct languages. Their communities are chiefly in Idaho, Colorado, Utah, Nevada, and northern Arizona. In the 1960s a population of about 12,000 lived on 22 federal reservations and 6 colonies. For the most part these peoples lack the large-scale cohesive organization and complex religious and social life of the northern plains peoples. Two of the groups—the Paiutes and the Shoshones—are widely scattered in small communities, both on and off reservations, and probably do not share a common sense of identity. Their history and their situation in the 1960s are rather different from those of any of the plains peoples. The Nez Perce and the Utes living on federal reservations are more concentrated. The Utes are on three different reservations and maintain the largest Indian communities of the region.

Nez Perces

The Nez Perces continue to bear the name given them by French fur traders, referring to the custom of piercing their noses for the insertion of ornaments. They belong to the Sahaptin language family, in contrast to the other peoples of the region, who speak languages of the Shoshonean branch of the Uto-Aztecan stock. The Nez Perces number more than 1,500, a reduction of about 2,500 since their first contact with whites. The great majority live on a reservation in northern Idaho; less than a hundred live on the Colville Reservation in Washington.

The Nez Perces, despite their distinctive language, are culturally typical of the northern Rocky Mountains region. Before being forced into reservation life, they lived in small independent bands and subsisted by hunting, gathering, and salmon fishing. By the 1730s they had obtained horses from their former enemies, the Shoshones, a development that enhanced their traditional nomadism and made them partly reliant on buffalo hunting in the plains. They alone among Indians developed selective breeding of horses, resulting in the Appaloosa. The Nez Perce adopted many traits of the northern Plains Indians, although not the more complex religious ceremonials or the strong political organization.

Having heard something of Christianity from their early contacts with the French, in 1831 the Nez Perce sent a delegation to St. Louis to request books and teachers. Presbyterian and later Catholic missionaries arrived, and most of the tribe became Christians, chiefly Presbyterians, but in the late 1840s, as white settlers moved into their area, they became disaffected with the missionaries, who nevertheless remained active. In 1852 the Union Pacific Railroad was surveyed through Nez Perce country, and the Indians were divested of their land in the usual way. In 1855 a treaty was signed by separate Nez Perce headmen, ceding a large part of their land, and the main body of the tribe was forced into a portion of its former hunting territory, from which a reservation was formed in central Idaho.

One group in the Wallowa Valley of northeastern Oregon, whose headmen had not signed the treaty, refused to move. At first the federal government allowed this, but pressures from white settlers resulted in conflict, and eventually the government decision was reversed. Finally military action was taken against the group, and Nez Perce, settlers, and cavalrymen were killed. Forcible removal of all Nez Perces to the Idaho reservation was attempted, but the Wallowa group resisted and tried to escape to Canada. Their retreat of more than 1,000 miles—in its last phase under the leadership of Heinmot Tooyalakekt, or, as the whites called him, Chief Joseph (c. 1840–1904)—became famous all over the United States. Chief Joseph's speech, when he was finally captured in 1877, gave currency to the concept of the "vanishing American" and was very widely quoted. As the bulk of Nez Perces settled into reservation life in Idaho, Chief Joseph and some 400 followers were shipped to Fort Leavenworth, Kans., and then to Indian Territory, where many died. Settlers near the Nez Perce reservation in Idaho were so strongly opposed to Chief Joseph's return that the government decided to send him instead to the Colville Reservation in Washington territory, where a miscellaneous group of Indians was assembling.

The Nez Perces on the reservation were furnished rations for a time and turned to stock raising and some farming. The BIA agent required them to cut their traditionally long hair and to wear conventional American-style clothing. The agent appointed a tribal chief and subchiefs, who were paid salaries until 1880. From 1875 to 1895 the Presbyterians were the most powerful force on the reservation. They opposed all aspects of traditional life—ceremonies, gambling games, dances, and curing rites—and made a deliberate effort to curb the authority of the traditional headmen and the ordaining of native ministers, of which there were a dozen by 1893. They also put the Sahaptin language into written form and published all their religious literature in that language. The BIA agent worked closely only with the Presbyterians, so an opposition Catholic group supported a Catholic chief, and the foundations of a strong factional split were laid.

Between 1890 and 1895 the reservation was allotted, despite the opposition of the Nez Perces; more than two-thirds of the land was declared surplus and promptly went into white hands. In 1892, through the efforts of the BIA agent, a nine-man committee of Presbyterians was formed to solve the problems caused by allotment. By 1923 one-half of the remaining land had been sold, with the result that the majority of the Nez Perces were forced into wage labor for white farmers and ranchers or in the towns of the region.

By the 1960s their way of life had become barely distinguishable from that of white neighbors. Most Indian children attend public schools, and there has been much intermarriage, so few Nez Perces claimed to be full-bloods. Most of the mixture is with whites, but there are some intertribal marriages, chiefly with other plateau tribes. By 1963 more than 25 percent of the Nez Perces lived off the reservation, many in the immediate vicinity.

Since 1940 there has been considerable participation in two evangelical denominations—the Assembly of God and the Church of God. After the introduction of these white-controlled churches, three independent evangelical sects arose that were managed entirely by Nez Perces. The independent evangelicals are especially interested in the second coming and the millennial doctrines of these denominations. The tendency to religious schism, begun by the Nez Perce Presbyterians, has continued strongly.

The Nez Perce tribe continues to exist as a distinct political entity. The rival Presbyterian and Catholic chieftainships of the 1870s showed a strong interest in organized leadership and a capacity for political organization, which continued into the 20th century. The committee on allotment was revived in 1923—this time with one Catholic member—when the BIA instituted a five-year economic development plan. The committee functioned in conjunction with an all-male general assembly. A constitution was written and approved by the BIA, which established the committee as the official body for handling leasing and other business matters. With this organization functioning, the Nez Perces rejected reorganization under the IRA in 1934.

However, many young men returning from the armed services in 1948 regarded the committee as too much dominated by the BIA and wrote a new constitution, which established the Nez Perce Tribal Executive Committee as the dominant political body. The former general assembly no longer functioned. The NPTEC has remained a focus of vigorous political interest and has stimulated the formation of political parties. In the 1950s the Warriors, a group favoring the revival of traditional ceremonies and gaming activities and opposing the 1948 constitution, was active. In the 1960s that group disappeared, but a new organization, the Nez Perce Indian Association, composed of off-reservation Indians, continued to oppose the constitution. Its rival is another new organization, largely of reservation-dwellers, called the Loyal Nez Perces, which actively supports the constitution and also the revival of traditional ways.

Utes

In their history and present situation, the Utes somewhat resemble the Nez Perces. The Utes lived in the eastern Rocky Mountain area and acquired horses before 1675, somewhat earlier than the Nez Perces because the Utes were closer to the supply in New Mexico. They also hunted the buffalo, but to a lesser degree than did the Nez Perces, because they were kept out of the plains region by Comanches and then by Cheyennes and Arapahos. The Utes engaged in little warfare with whites, although in 1855, under pressure of the advancing settlers, they joined with the Jicarilla Apaches in brief opposition and were defeated. From that time they did not organize for warfare but lived either in isolation or at the edges of white settlements in New Mexico, Colorado, and Utah. Their numbers were reduced from perhaps 4,500 in the early 19th century to about 2,500 in 1960.

Originally inhabiting central and western Colorado, eastern Utah, and northeastern New Mexico, they were reduced to the Uintah and Ouray reservation in northeastern Utah and the Southern Ute and Ute Mountain reservations in southwestern Colorado. Like many of the tribes of the Rockies area, they were not forced onto reservations until the 1880s.

The contrasts among the different groups are exemplified on the Colorado reservations, on each of which there are about 500 Utes. The Ute Mountain Band has an unallotted, closed reservation held in common under federal trust. They are somewhat nomadic, many following their sheep to different locations and living in tents or intermittently in cabins. Most are members of the Native American church and all practice the traditional ceremonial Bear Dance. Few of the older people speak English; the Ute language is spoken in most homes. The Ute Mountain Utes lived largely on rations until 1931. After that they supported themselves largely by raising sheep or working for wages at the BIA agency. They had no tribal council under the IRA, instead living by the traditional headman authority system.

In contrast, Utes on the Southern Ute Reservation live on individually held land and are largely small-scale farmers. English is generally spoken, and their houses are like those of neighboring whites, but both hair styles and clothing are traditional. They have a tribal council organized under the provisions of the IRA. The Peyote rites have been strong since 1917, although probably most Utes also belong to Christian churches. The tribal Bear Dance is an important annual event.

Shoshones and Paiutes

Small communities of Shoshones and Paiutes are scattered through Utah, Nevada, southern Idaho, and northwestern Arizona. In addition, Shoshones live on two large reservations, one in Wyoming and one in southeastern Idaho, and Paiutes live on a reservation in Nevada. The Shoshones in Idaho share the Fort Hall Reservation with the Bannocks, another Shoshonean-speaking people; and the Shoshones of the Wind River Reservation in Wyoming share theirs with the northern Arapahos. About 4,000, or more than 40 percent of the Shoshones and Paiutes, live in the region but off the reservations; some of these groups are called colonies and have arrangements for services, such as health care, with the federal government. The population on the larger reservations of both Shoshones and Paiutes is about 5,000.

The situation of the reservation Shoshones is little different from that of the Nez Perces and Utes on the allotted reservations. The adoption of white ways is well advanced, especially with regard to occupations, housing, clothing, and other aspects of material culture; most are Christians. Tribal councils under IRA provisions govern the reservations. A distinct sense of Indian identity has been fostered by the possession of some land under tribal trust and the prosecution of claims through the Indian Claims Commission. The sense of tribal identity is perhaps strongest among the Wind River Shoshones, the Fort Hall Northern Shoshones, and the White Knife Shoshones of the Duck Valley Reservation in Idaho and Nevada. They are also active in intertribal pow-wows and have adopted much of the ceremonial symbolism of those circuits.

The thousands of other Paiutes and Western Shoshones of Nevada, Utah, and Arizona have a history either of peaceful relations with whites as they advanced into this inhospitable region or of occasional attacks on wagon trains. Because of their lack of overt hostility and the widely scattered and never centrally organized character of their life, they were largely ignored by the whites, except for an occasional massacre in retaliation for pilfering. Most of the scattered Paiutes, Utes, and Shoshones became laborers in the towns or domestics and ranch hands on the ranches that slowly grew up in the region.

In the late 1880s Wovoka (c. 1856–1932), the originator and messiah of the Ghost Dance religion, became widely influential. He was a Walker River Paiute of a very peaceful group, but his vision of the disappearance of the whites was clearly indicative of the underlying resistance to white culture, which was probably as strong among individual Paiutes as among any organized groups that fought against white domination. Wovoka's tradition of leadership continued among the Walker River Paiutes into the 1960s. For example, the National Indian Youth Council, organized by "young Turks" within the National Congress of American Indians in the 1960s, derived its leadership from Paiutes as well as from Oklahoma Poncas.

THE SOUTHWEST

The Indian population of New Mexico and Arizona is unique in a number of respects. During the 1960s the Southwest had the largest number of Indians of any region in the United States, although this has not always been true. The population of approximately 217,000 in these two states is nearly three times what it was during the period of Spanish conquest in the 1500s and 1600s. The increase has been especially rapid during the 20th century because of the growth of a single tribal group, the Navajos. The other groups are either below or only slightly above their numbers at the time of first contact with Europeans.

The Southwest is also characterized by a large number of Indian ethnic groups, more than there are in any other geographic area. There were in the 1960s about 40 groups that regarded themselves as distinct from one another. Some tribal extinctions have occurred—three tribes that lived along the lower Colorado River, perhaps three that lived in the Rio Grande Valley, and two or three others. These extinctions are balanced by increases resulting from the creation of new identities through the establishment of separate reservations for groups that were formerly unified and the arrival of Indian groups new to the area.

To a far greater extent than anywhere else in the United States, the Indian groups in the Southwest have maintained their own customs, ways and fundamental values and have selectively borrowed cultural elements from Europeans and others. This does not mean that the Indian cultures have not changed but rather that the government programs of forced assimilation have not worked so effectively here and that the Indian communities have been less penetrated by whites than elsewhere. Indian ways of life are more readily recognizable as such in this region, and their cultural orientations remain more clearly distinctive.

Several circumstances have contributed to this situation. One of great importance is that the native peoples here were not forced to move as much from their home areas nor were they forced to cede vast territory. Not until the late 20th century did the pressures for appropriation of Indian land, water, and mineral resources become as intense as they had been 150 years earlier in the rest of the country. By that time federal Indian policy had changed radically, and Indian organization had developed to the point that it is possible that the experience of other Indians will not be repeated in this part of the United States. The phase of wholesale expropriation of Indian lands may have passed.

The Eastern Pueblos

In the 1960s there were about 8,500 people along the Rio Grande in New Mexico whom whites lumped together as Pueblos, a collective term that these people have also adopted. This population is made up of 16 distinct groups that live in communities quite separate from one another, maintaining their own very distinct identities. Each uses as the language of the home one or another dialect of four different language groups—Tewa, Tiwa, Keresan, and Towa. The communities in which they live consist of contiguous masonry or adobe houses built around plazas in very much the same plan as when the Spaniards first saw them in 1540. Some houses are built in stepped two-, three-, or even four-story arrangements, following a regional apartment-house style that is at least 700 years old. The houses also have window glass, hinged doors, and other such additions from white culture, representing a selective borrowing characteristic of the Pueblos in most aspects of life. Each community practices its own native religious ceremonies, which are centered in partially underground buildings called *kivas*. Nearly every community also has a Catholic church, supplementing the elaborate ceremonies of the native religion. The Native American church has members in only one village.

All the Pueblo communities are characterized by a local governmental organization that combines the traditional hereditary offices with some offices introduced by the Spanish. This local government operates in conjunction with a general assembly. Three of the Pueblo communities, in addition, have IRA-based tribal councils that cooperate with the BIA agency in Albuquerque. Also the communities elect representatives to an all-Pueblo council that deliberates regularly on matters of collective concern.

The religious ceremonies are vigorously maintained, and nearly everyone in a village participates. The economic life combines farming and some stock raising, and most villages have active workers in pottery, textiles, and other crafts. There are a number of painters and some sculptors who combine native traditional subject matter with Western artistic traditions, and whose works are bought by the general public.

In 1540 the Eastern Pueblos accepted Spanish political control and Franciscan missionaries reluctantly after some resistance; they remained peaceful until 1680, when they united in a revolt against the Spaniards, resulting in the killing or ousting of all Spaniards from their country. They were reconquered in 1695–1697, but they succeeded in keeping the Christian missionaries at arm's length by allowing them to build churches at the edges of their communities, while continuing their own religion in secrecy. They integrated elements of the administration required by the Spaniards with their own community organization. From the time of the reconquest they remained peaceful and found effective ways to limit the efforts of both Spaniards and Americans to alter their way of life.

The Rio Grande Pueblo people joined with the Spaniards during the 1700s and early 1800s in military resistance to raids by the surrounding nomadic tribes, such as the Navajos and Apaches. There was an intricate interweaving of Indian and European culture traits in most aspects of life, but never cultural dominance by the Spaniards. The Spanish and Mexican colonists also assimilated many Indian cultural traits. During the 1920s the Pueblos successfully withstood legal efforts by New Mexicans to reduce their land, a result of concerted effort by an all-Pueblo council, the first common organization since 1680.

The Pueblos suffered less loss of land than most other western Indians and also succeeded in blocking to some extent the efforts of the BIA to assimilate them culturally. Nevertheless, they send their children to schools and have steadily became bilingual. During the post-IRA period one of their languages, Tewa, was given written form by the Bureau of Indian Affairs and was used for a time in the federal schools serving the Tewa-speakers. Also the BIA instituted a special school to train Indians in Indian arts, which encouraged new creative developments and national recognition of Indian artists. During the 1960s the Pueblos, with federal aid, instituted programs for the development of native arts and built museums to encourage interest in their traditions.

Western Pueblos

Five groups, the Hopis, Hopi-Tewas, Zunis, Acomas, and Lagunas, whose way of life is generally similar to that of the Rio Grande Pueblos, live in western New Mexico and northeastern Arizona; they numbered about 12,000 in the 1960s. Each group lives in masonry Pueblo-type towns or groups of towns, including smaller satellite communities. The Acoma and Hopi villages are situated on the tops of mesas.

The Hopis, the largest of the western Pueblos in Arizona, with about 5,000 population, almost entirely escaped lasting influence by the Spanish and the early missionaries. Some of their present villages are dated by tree rings as having been built at least as early as the 14th century. According to their myths they emerged from the ground at a place called Sipapu on the Little Colorado River. They then wandered in the region for centuries before settling in their present locations. They joined in the 1680 revolt against the Spaniards and following that were successful in keeping Franciscan and other missionaries out of their villages by, for example, destroying one Hopi community that favored the return of the Spaniards. Thus the culture that they have preserved into the 20th century lacks the strong Spanish influence apparent among the Rio Grande Pueblos.

During the late 19th and 20th centuries Mennonite and Baptist missionaries gained converts among the Hopis, while the Zunis, along with the Acomas and Lagunas, came under Catholic and Dutch Reformed influences. Most of the western Pueblos practice the native religion, centering on the kivas and emphasizing belief in the *kachinas*, ancestral spirits who are represented in masked dances during the spring and summer. The religion requires an exacting round of ceremonial observances for most villagers. Religious leadership is along hereditary lines in certain clans, and all adult males are initiated into the kachina society.

All of the western Pueblos have tribal councils according to IRA regulations. Among the Hopis the institution of the council gave rise to vigorous opposition from residents of the two western groups of villages, who believed that such organization was contrary to sacred prophecy. However, the council has continued to grow in acceptance and influence and has won favorable settlements before the Indian Claims Commission.

Apaches

In the 1960s four groups bore the name of Apache, two on New Mexico and two on Arizona reservations. Together they numbered 9,229, some 3,000 to 4,000 more than in the 1600s when they were first encountered by the Spaniards. Some cultural traits of the Jicarillas in northern New Mexico, such as their use of tipis, reflect their life on the plains during the 17th and early 18th centuries. But in most respects all the Apaches are similar: they live in frame houses and wear American-style clothing and are for the most part stock raisers; the Western Apaches of Arizona occupy some of the finest cattle-grazing land in the state. Their native religion, which has not been highly organized, persists in the form of curing rituals and rites for adolescent girls and as elements in new religions that they have adopted. Most are nominally Catholics, Lutherans, or members of evangelical Protestant denominations. Beginning in the 1950s the Mormons and the Assembly of God gained Apache converts. The Assembly of God has been especially successful among the Western Apaches, as among the Nez Perces and some Plains peoples. There are also some independent Protestant denominations that seceded from Lutheran and other denominations over the issue of Apache control of the ministry. In addition there is a synthetic new religion that follows the ideas of a Western Apache called Silas John, which combines Catholic, Protestant, and, above all, native Apache rituals. Apaches are active in pan-Indian pow-wows and in the National Congress of American Indians.

The use of the Apache language in the home is widespread. In the 1960s a movement developed among the Western Apaches for reviving the language and reducing it to writing; that had already been done by Lutheran missionaries, but the new effort was conceived and carried out by Apaches. In their religious life, especially in the Assembly of God and the Silas John movement, Apaches have sought to manage their own affairs and reject white controls. Apaches are active in the arts, particularly in sculpture and painting. Alan Hauser was nationally prominent as a painter.

All the Apaches organized tribal councils under the provisions of the IRA and have actively participated in the resulting political organization. Through their councils they prosecute suits before the Indian Claims Commission and manage cattle industries and other tribal economic enterprises.

Their tribal history is important to the Apaches, and they generally hold that it has not been written correctly, despite the large number of publications on the subject. The Apache point of view is usually omitted, they believe, or misrepresented. For example, they do not accept the well-known Apache leader Geronimo (1829–1909) as an adequate symbol of their recent past, but regard his reputation as a white invention.

The Apaches came into the Southwest probably not before the 15th or 16th century, having been pushed into the region from farther north and east by Comànches, Kiowas, and Eastern Apaches. The Western Apaches, consisting of the ancestors of the San Carlos, White Mountain, and Chiricahua groups, moved in first, followed by the Mescaleros and Jicarillas. One incentive was the opportunity to obtain horses from the Spanish settlers who were invading New Mexico and what became Arizona and Sonora, Mexico. The Apaches developed a way of life that depended heavily on raiding for horses and provisions. They never bred horses but used them for greater mobility in raiding, and often they ate their flesh. They became well adapted to a life of periodic raiding and participated in the slave trade stimulated by the Spaniards during the 1700s. Between 1685 and the late 1700s the Apaches were successful in slowing down the Spanish occupation of the region. The Spaniards were unable to control Apache raiding, and in desperation they offered bounties for their scalps. They also tried to attract the Apaches to settle peacefully in the vicinity of presidios, or forts, giving them liquor, food, and clothing, but most Apaches remained hostile and were never converted to Christianity.

When the United States, under the stimulus of the Texans, invaded northern Mexico in 1845 and ultimately obtained New Mexico, Arizona, and California by conquest, it regarded the Apaches as conquered subjects; however, the Apaches regarded themselves as allies of the United States in a common war against the Mexicans and therefore resisted being forced on to reservations. The result was a long period of uncontrolled hostilities between them and the American settlers and miners of southwestern New Mexico and central and southeastern Arizona. The campaign to assemble all the Apaches on three reservations in southern Arizona and New Mexico was costly and went on for 20 years, from 1866 to 1886, under different commanders of the U.S. Cavalry. Nearly all the Apaches had begun to settle on the reservations and to allow themselves to be divided up into tagbands or ration-receiving groups by the time Geronimo and some other individuals became prominent through their breakaways from the reservations. By 1887 all the Apaches were finally gathered on the reservations, the raiding ceased, and they began a total reorganization of their lives. Geronimo and his Chiricahua followers were sent to Indian Territory.

The BIA was unwilling to allow the Apaches sufficient

freedom to hunt and gather food in their accustomed ways. Rations were issued for more than 20 years as Apaches were forced into the new concentrations of population. Slowly some farming and stock raising were introduced; others did wage work on the large irrigation dams, such as the Roosevelt Dam in Arizona. It was not until the 1940s, when land was placed back in Apache hands after years of the BIA leasing it to white cattle companies, that the basic new Apache economy began to take hold. By the 1950s Apaches were well established in the cattle industry and did not experience the setbacks suffered by the northern Plains tribes. The Apache reservations have never been allotted but are held in common under trust with the federal government.

Western Apaches did not pay much attention to the Ghost Dance religion, and new religious ways did not arise among them until the 1930s. In the late 1920s they began to be interested in the teachings of Silas John, a White Mountain Apache who had been a Roman Catholic. The Silas John movement continued to grow for the next 50 years, despite the jailing of the prophet, and was maintained along with the developing independent Protestant churches managed by Apaches.

Navajos

More than any tribe in the United States, the Navajos have increased their numbers since first contacts with whites. In 1868, when a treaty was made between the Navajos and the U.S. government, there were between 8,000 and 9,000 Navajos; by 1975 the estimate had risen to about 160,000, making them by far the largest single tribe in the country. The great majority live on the largest reservation in the United States, which is chiefly in Arizona but overlaps into New Mexico and Utah.

The Navajos also have the largest tribal income in the United States—approximately $50 million in 1970, largely from oil and gas leases and royalties and returns from other mineral and forest resources. The tribe as a business corporation is engaged in various enterprises, ranging from the manufacture and sale of arts and crafts to the production of lumber. However, many Navajos live far below the poverty level. These economic contrasts indicate the great variations that characterize Navajo life generally.

The Navajo Nation, as it is officially designated, has a democratically elected tribal council, which existed before the passage of the IRA in 1934, but has never been reorganized in accord with that act. The Navajo Nation has never ratified a constitution, but its political organization functions essentially like those of tribes organized under the IRA and has progressively taken over governmental functions from the BIA during the 1970s.

Navajos work in a variety of occupations, with wage work both on and off the reservation the source of the greater part of individual income. Sheep raising and construction work are important, and several kinds of industries have moved onto the reservation, while the tribal administration manages a sawmill and the manufacture of other forest products. Irrigation farming is important on several parts of the reservation, as is coal mining. The tribe manages a tribal park service and a fish and game department. In many respects the tribal government functions like a state government, always with the special assistance of federal aid, especially in the maintenance of schools and in medical services.

The Navajo Nation during the 1960s started, with the help of governmental and private foundation funds, a special experimental school on the reservation. The aim of the Rough Rock Demonstration School is to bring Navajo cultural traditions into school programs so that they can play an important role in childhood learning and development. The Navajo language is used in instruction, and tribal information is gathered from older Navajo-speaking men and women for instructional purposes. In addition the tribal council inaugurated with private and public funds the Navajo Community College, a junior college in which

Navajo Studies, including the language, tribal history, and elements of their culture, are the core of the curriculum.

Navajos are members of a wide variety of churches— Roman Catholic, Episcopal, Baptist, Assembly of God, Mormon, Church of the Nazarene, Native American church (Peyote cult), and many others. The Peyote cult gained adherents rapidly during the 1960s and 1970s, although the tribal council passed legislation against the use of peyote. The native Navajo religion continues to be strong among a majority, with curing aspects the special focus of interest. The Navajos speak an Athapaskan language, very close to that of the Western Apaches. It is spoken as the language of the home by probably a majority on the reservation.

The Navajos probably separated from the plains-dwelling Athapaskans as early as the 12th century and came into contact with Pueblo Indians in the region of the upper Rio Grande drainage. Traditional Navajo belief holds that they originated in the region in which they were living when Europeans first encountered them in the 1600s; the traditional region of origin is marked by four mountain peaks in Arizona, New Mexico, Colorado, and Utah. During the Pueblo revolt against the Spaniards in 1680 many Pueblos came to live with them, and the Navajos borrowed much from the Pueblos culturally, especially religious beliefs and rituals. They also borrowed important elements of material life from the Spaniards, although only a tiny percentage of Navajos ever came into close contact with them. Through trading and raiding they borrowed the techniques of silver-making and weaving, as well as the use of sheep and horses, and as a result of these resources the Navajos became a herding culture during the 17th and 18th centuries. They remained at the periphery of Spanish society in New Mexico, unlike the Rio Grande Pueblos, who were in the center of it.

When the United States invaded New Mexico and the area to the west during the Mexican War, the Navajos did not accept U.S. control. In 1864 nearly every Navajo was rounded up and made to walk, under the direction of the U.S. Army, 800 miles northeast to Fort Sumner, N.Mex., where the government proposed to make farmers out of the herders and hunters. The plan failed completely, many Navajos died, and ultimately the government agreed to allow the 8,000 Navajos to walk back to their old territory, where a reservation was set up and a treaty was made in which the Navajos agreed to be peaceful and the U.S. government promised to set up schools and provide other services and means of livelihood. The march to and from Fort Sumner, in the course of which there was much suffering, became known in Navajo tradition as the Long Walk.

Once back in Arizona Territory, they engaged in sheepherding, which steadily became their major means of livelihood; the blankets they wove from the wool began to be known across the United States. In the 1930s, however, the technicians of the Soil Conservation Service decided that the range on the reservation was being seriously depleted and that in order to save it, Navajo stock—sheep, horses, and goats—would have to be drastically reduced. Stock reduction was carried out amid Navajo pleas that their sole means of livelihood was being destroyed. Deep hostility and distrust of government resulted, and this event, like the Long Walk, assumed a prominent place in Navajo history.

During the 1960s the Office of Economic Opportunity instituted a large-scale training program in community development techniques, which gave thousands of Navajos a chance to participate in government on a scale they had not practiced before. Prior to this, the Bureau of Indian Affairs had encouraged local community organizations known as chapters. By the 1970s the foundation was laid for widespread individual participation in Navajo government at the local group level, as well as at the level of the tribal council. The Navajos by 1975 were participating in American society in a great variety of ways and were at the same time placing a high value on their own language and tribal traditions.

Pais

The Pais consist of several bands of people who speak closely related dialects of a Yuman language and live at the southwestern edge of the Colorado Plateau in what is now northwestern Arizona. By the 1970s the Pais had been divided into four different groups and placed on six reservations. Their population was about 1,800; the largest groups, the Hualapai, numbered about 800. A smaller group of about 400 have come to be known as the Havasupai and live on a separate reservation at the bottom of Cataract Canyon, immediately west of the Grand Canyon, on the Colorado River. These two, constituting the majority of Pai-speaking peoples, were very closely associated until the late 19th century, but the creation of reservations in the 1880s led to the development of somewhat separate identities by the 1970s, and whites regarded them as entirely distinct peoples.

Most of the Hualapais (or Walapais) live near Peach Springs in northwestern Arizona, where the BIA has established an agency. The Hualapai Indian Nation has a nine-member tribal council and a tribal court system organized in 1939 under the regulations of the IRA. Like most other southwestern Indian peoples, the Hualapai Tribe manages a number of enterprises, including a thriving herd of cattle, a doll manufacturing business, a trading company, a housing authority, and a wildlife department. In addition to cattle raising, many men work on the railroad. They belong to various Christian churches but also maintain interest in older Hualapai ceremonial dances and songs and participate annually in pow-wows and intertribal ceremonials. Most speak Hualapai in the home, but interest is declining on the part of young people, who speak English as a result of their schooling. Frame, masonry, or concrete-block houses have entirely replaced the former frame wickiups. Clothing is of the western ranch type, except for long full dresses worn by many middle-aged and older women.

The Havasupais, who live on a reservation 60 miles northeast of the Peach Springs agency, developed in somewhat different ways from the Hualapais. Until the 1950s they lived in what had been a relatively inaccessible area, at the bottom of a steep-walled canyon. Their location contrasts with that of the Hualapais at Peach Springs, through which have been built the Santa Fe Railroad in the 1880s and the most traveled highway across the United States. As a result of their inaccessibility, the Havasupais were better able to fend off the efforts of the BIA and others seeking to change their way of life. Various churches, from Mormon to Episcopal and Baptist, tried but failed to establish themselves among the Havasupais. Although efforts were made to introduce frame houses, the Havasupais used them for storage and continued to live in their traditional brush wickiups most of the year. However, during the 1970s they began to use the ranch-style houses built by the BIA. All families speak the Pai language at home, and most are bilingual. At one time Havasupai life was divided between the canyon, where they farmed by irrigation and maintained peach orchards, and the plateau 5,000 feet above, where they raised cattle and horses. During the 20th century Havasupais learned to make their living through tourism, first at the Grand Canyon and later by conducting tours into their own highly scenic canyon. They organized a tribal council and adopted a constitution in 1938, under IRA regulations, through which they manage a tribal cafe, store, and tourist enterprise. The tribe also manages the Native American Education Program and a tribal library and archive. Tourist-related jobs are probably the chief source of livelihood, except for farming on the canyon bottom and raising some livestock on the plateau.

Pai contacts with Spaniards and Mexicans were for the most part indirect. They were not conquered by the Spanish, but through them, via the Hopis, they became familiar with metal, cattle, horses, peaches, apricots, and melon production, and woolen blankets and clothing. The Pais had practiced irrigated agriculture before the coming of the Europeans. Intensive contacts with whites did not begin before the mid-19th century and were at first chiefly clashes with military exploring parties. As miners and then cattlemen made encroachments on their land, all bands of Pais resisted, and fighting began. The Havasupais, however, gradually retired from the conflict to their canyon and figured very little in the hostilities. The Hualapais, however, fought hard and gained a reputation for courage and fighting ability. By 1866 the U.S. government, freed of the military demands of the Civil War, sent cavalry in considerable numbers into Arizona Territory to protect the many miners and ranchers who had moved into the Indian country without treaty or arrangement. What was called the Walapai War was fought against both the Hualapais and the Yavapais to the south between 1866 and 1869. When Hualapais were ultimately subdued, they joined the Americans against their traditional enemies, the Yavapais. In 1874 the government decided to eliminate completely the Hualapais from the mountain country by sending all they could round up to La Paz on the east side of the Colorado River in the lowland desert country, where they would be more manageable. During the relocation, many died or became sick; they tried to escape and were brought back. Eventually, in 1875, after being moved again, the Hualapais broke away and returned in small groups to their old hunting territories. The Havasupais had been overlooked entirely, remaining undisturbed in their vast canyon.

Having to accept rations from the government on their now-restricted territories, the Hualapais steadily lost hope as they lost independence. In 1889 they embraced the Ghost Dance, with its promise of a future life of the old free kind, but when the whites did not disappear in a few years, they turned to cooperation with them and accepted reservation life as cattlemen.

Reservations were created in the 1880s for all the Pai people, the Havasupais and Hualapais being located in very small parts of their former territories, the Yavapais on a tiny acreage at Camp Verde, Ariz., on another small reservation at Fort McDowell near Phoenix, and with Apaches on the

San Carlos Apache Reservation farther east. One small group of Yavapais maintained residence at Prescott, but had no federal recognition or trust land until the 1960s.

Pimas and Papagos

Like the Pais, the Piman-speaking peoples of southern Arizona are another group whose political organization and distribution on reservations does not reflect their original affiliations. Although they all speak dialects of the same Uto-Aztecan language, whites have come to think of them as two distinct peoples—Pimas and Papagos—because of the naming of the reservations that were carved out of their land. In the valley of the Gila River south of Phoenix is the Gila River Reservation, where the Indians were called Pimas or Pimos by the white immigrants who encountered them in the mid-19th century. Farther south are three very small reservations —the Akchin, the Gila Bend, and the San Xavier—and one very large one, the Sells, all of which are the homes of people regarded by whites as Papagos. Other Piman-speakers also live there, and all, along with the Pimas of the Gila River Reservation, speak mutually intelligible dialects of the widely distributed language that the Spaniards called Pima.

In 1970 the Papagos on their four reservations numbered somewhat less than 15,000, the Pimas on their two reservations about 11,000. In addition at least another 2,500, who identify themselves as Papagos, are scattered in communities of southern Arizona. Thus the total Pima-speaking population of Arizona on and off reservations is in the neighborhood of 29,000–30,000—currently one of the larger tribes of the United States and probably more than three times the population of the area at the beginning of European contacts.

Three of the Papago reservations, although 60 and 75 miles apart, are organized into a single political structure—the Papago Tribe—and participate in the Papago Tribal Council with a constitution approved by the BIA under the IRA. The council, with funds from various government sources and with tribal income from cattle sales and mining royalties, manages some 30 enterprises, ranging from a tribal herd to a comprehensive employment training program. The council also sponsors an annual rodeo and fair and a Miss Papago contest and manages an arts and crafts production and sales center and a utility authority. In some of these enterprises the administrative responsibilities are shared with the BIA.

Papagos are members of Catholic, Presbyterian, Baptist, Methodist, or Assembly of God churches. The largest number belong to the Catholic church, which has maintained Franciscan missionaries among the Pima-speaking people since the late 1700s and Jesuits before that for nearly a century. Most of the more than 70 villages in which Papagos live maintain their own small churches, with a style of worship sometimes called Sonoran Catholic, which is a folk version of Catholicism oriented around St. Francis Xavier, the patron of the Jesuits. In 1970 only a minority of families spoke Papago in their homes, but at least 80 percent of Papagos were bilingual in English and Papago.

The Papagos have maintained a tribal organization embracing the whole group only since the IRA. Groups of villages had organized in 1695 and again in 1750 to resist the Spaniards and their program of military and missionary domination. The 1750 revolt led by Oacpicagigua was a serious threat to the Spaniards for a year, but after that, resistance gave way to an extended period of peaceful cooperation with Spaniards, Mexicans, and finally Anglo-Americans. When the Western Apaches raided Spanish and Mexican ranches, the Papagos fought with Spaniards and later the white settlers against them. But their cooperativeness did not help the Papagos in combating the intensified white encroachments as mines and ranches were opened up during the last years of the 19th century.

It was not until 1917 that the large Papago reservation was established, covering much of the land the desert Papagos had ranged over; in contrast, the river Papagos, living where whites began to concentrate after 1900, were forced to accept only a tiny portion of their territory around the Spanish mission of St. Francis Xavier. Marked rural-urban contrasts exist between Papagos living in the many villages scattered over the desert country and those living in the major concentration at Sells. Government-planned housing near Sells, resembling the suburban tracts in Arizona cities, contrasts with the small adobe houses and shade structures in the villages. As the Papago population has grown, thousands have found jobs in Arizona cities, and a permanent city group has formed; the city-dwellers, however, are linked through kinship and regular visiting with the reservation communities.

The Papagos after World War II became preeminent in basket-making, developing new forms and patterns of decoration based on the traditional styles. Their baskets have gained a national market and are exhibited and sold at intertribal gatherings everywhere in the United States. In their music and art, in contrast, they tend to borrow from rather than influence other Indian groups.

The Pima situation is basically similar to that of the Papagos. They have had an effectively functioning tribal council with an elected governor and representatives since the 1930s. The tribe as a business corporation is similarly engaged in numerous business and industrial enterprises, manages a tribal farm and herd of cattle, and sponsors a tribal museum, a regionally well-known arts and crafts center, and other activities. Pimas are chiefly Presbyterians and Catholics and to a greater extent than the Papagos have lost traditional forms of religious expression. However, there is some revival of traditional crafts, pottery, and basket-making, and ceremonial dance.

Like the Papagos, they maintained mostly friendly relations with the Spaniards and Anglo-Americans. Under the peaceful leadership of Antonio Azul, they sold food to the wagon trains that began to pass through their country in the mid-19th century. Despite their friendly assistance, Anglo-American settlers, from the 1880s into the 20th century, appropriated almost all the water from the Gila River, which their villages had relied on for 2,000 years. They still use to some extent the system of irrigation canals that their ancestors had laid out beginning in 300 B.C. By the 1950s the Pimas were unable to subsist by farming, at which time they brought a claim against the United States through the Indian Claims Commission. As water storage facilities were developed there was some relief, but only small-scale agriculture was possible.

Mohaves, Chemehuevis, and Cuchans

In the 1960s three groups of Yuman-speaking peoples—Mohaves, Chemehuevis, and Cuchans—lived on reservations in the lower Colorado River Valley. Their total population of about 2,350 represents a considerable reduction from about 150 years ago, when there were seven Yuman-speaking groups with a population of at least 13,000. Three groups have become extinct, and one—the Maricopas—was forced to take refuge on the Gila River Reservation. In 1970 about 200 Maricopas preserved their identity distinct from the Pimas in a single community.

Of the surviving groups, the Cuchans, commonly called Yumas, number 1,150 and live on one reservation at Fort Yuma in extreme southeastern California. They are organized as a business corporation and a tribe, farm much of their reservation, maintain important native ceremonials, and participate regularly in southwestern and other intertribal gatherings. Next largest are the Mohaves, who number about 900 and live on two reservations, one at Parker, Ariz., the other in Arizona and California, near Needles, Calif. Both groups of Mohaves, who identify separately, have tribal councils. The Parker political–administrative organization is known as the Colorado River Tribes. The Needles, or Fort Mohave, people live chiefly by wage work on the railroad. The Parker Mohaves possess excellent irrigated farmland, most of which they rent to non-Mohave farmers. They share the reservation land with some 300 Chemehuevis, a Shoshonean-speaking group, former residents of the desert lands to the west, and colonies of Navajos and Hopis who have been assigned land on the reservation.

Yaquis

Four major communities of Yaquis exist in Arizona—Guadalupe near Phoenix with 700, Old Pascua in Tucson with 500–600, New Pascua Pueblo near Tucson with 1,000–1,200, and Barrio Libre in South Tucson with an unestimated population. Scattered in the vicinity of these concentrations and elsewhere in southern Arizona are an estimated 2,500–3,000 Yaquis, making a total of between 5,000 and 6,000. Yaquis work in a wide variety of urban occupations and professions and to a lesser extent as agricultural laborers. Their houses and dress are like those of the urban dwellers among whom they live. All those who identify as Yaquis participate in distinctive Catholic-derived religious ceremonies in churches that the Yaquis maintain independently from Catholic church administration. The ceremonies are strongly Roman Catholic in character, but they are also strongly native American, especially with respect to two forms of ceremony—that of the Pascolas and the Deer Dancer, widely known in the region and in Mexico as distinctively Yaqui.

New Pascua Pueblo consists of communally owned land and is governed by a popularly elected tribal council. In 1978 New Pascua was formally recognized by the federal government, and the 200-acre tract on which the village is located became a reservation. Guadalupe was organized as an Arizona municipality, its city council having Yaqui as well as other representation. Old Pascua has an informal governing council, whose members are primarily holders of ceremonial offices, but the community also belongs to a neighborhood council organization. Barrio Libre, which has been divided by a freeway, has only a church-focused committee.

Yaquis in small numbers have lived in the southern Arizona region since the 1700s. In the 1890s their numbers were greatly increased when the regime of Porfirio Diaz forced hundreds of Yaquis from their traditional Mexican territory to the United States, where they were accorded the status of political refugees. Most Yaquis in Arizona in the 1970s were descendants of those refugees. Arizona and Mexican Yaquis communicate freely about their developments and problems.

Other Indians living in the Southwest in the 1970s were Paiutes and Utes.

CALIFORNIA

In the 1960s California had about 13,000 Indians, exclusive of those who lived in the large cities. The modern population may be considered survivors of early contacts with Europeans in the 17th and 18th centuries. Probably the most reasonable estimate of the total Indian population at the beginning of contact is 133,000, indicating a steady decline to less than one-tenth of the original population. From the founding of Spanish missions along the coast of southern California, beginning in 1769, to 1846, when California declared itself independent of Mexico, the Indian population declined rapidly by possibly one-half; this was a result of disease and poor living conditions in the mission communities of the south where they were forced to live. By the late 1840s the Indian population may have fallen to approximately 70,000. Then, as Anglo-Americans came for gold and land, a further precipitous drop took place: indiscriminate murder by whites, new epidemics, and displacement of whole communities resulted in a decline within 40 years to about 17,000.

Despite the precipitous decline in total population during the first 200 years, probably no more than one-quarter of the different groups became extinct. Possibly there were 40 language-culture groups among the original 133,000 popula-

tion, and in the 1960s the number of groups was 29. This figure must not be taken as indicating the maintenance of
strong Indian identity throughout the 200 years of intensive
contact. The Gabrielinos, who formerly occupied the area
that is now downtown Los Angeles, were completely dispersed, maintained no communities anywhere, and had totally lost their language and all distinctive cultural elements;
thus they could have been called extinct as a cultural group
before the middle of the 20th century or earlier. Yet when a
claims case began to be developed in the 1950s, 1,500 individuals presented genealogical credentials to qualify for a
share of the settlement. By the standard of sustaining a common community life, the Gabrielinos could be regarded as
extinct, but in terms of self-identification they are not. Of
the 29 mentioned above as distinct Indian ethnic groups, 9
number fewer than 100. To assume that groups so small are
necessarily on the verge of extinction has been demonstrated
many times to be unjustified; there have been instances in
which very small groups have intensified their sense of
identity and built new community structures rather than
moved toward disintegration.

The situation of the Indians in California is unique. Although the population density of the region's aboriginal cultures was perhaps the highest north of Mexico, no political
organization had developed beyond the level of the local
community. There were no strongly centralized tribal
groups capable of effective military organization or any intertribal confederacies exercising control over large regions,
such as those Europeans encountered in the East and in the
plains. California Indians lived in small villages that were
not linked with even their nearest neighbors for any common purposes except in some cases ceremonials or games.
Consequently, the incoming Europeans were faced with no
need for diplomatic maneuvers or military campaigns to establish political control. The result for the California natives
was chaos and destruction from the first.

The Spaniards began with Christian missions on the coast
of southern California in 1769. What began as voluntary in-

dividual conversion of the Indians ended as forced labor and forced cultural assimilation. The mission communities were built into large agricultural and industrial establishments into which Indians were forcibly recruited and kept under strict dormitory discipline. By the time Mexico won its independence (1821), tens of thousands of coastal Indians had been stripped of their culture and reoriented as lower-class laborers in Spanish society. The secularization of the missions that occurred under Mexican rule brought to the Indians not land and independence but more extreme dependence upon the Mexican landlords who took over.

The coming of the Anglo-Americans in 1848–1849 after the U.S. war with Mexico extended the Indians' condition of absolute subordination to the whole state. The newcomers were the extreme in frontiersmen, without respect for any law other than what they made themselves. The idea of Indian rights to land or to anything else was wholly foreign. Indians were murdered, plundered, pushed from what land they held, and then ignored in the constitutional government ultimately established (except for specific denial of the right to testify in court). The result was not only death and loss of property, but 75 years of social limbo, which no other Indians in the United States experienced. Despite efforts by a few reformers on behalf of white–Indian relations during the early 1850s, neither the federal government nor the state recognized the Indians' existence. They were not citizens, but neither were they wards of the state. The state appointed a superintendent of Indian affairs whose office did nothing, and the federal Bureau of Indian Affairs took no responsibility. The result was steady separation of Indians from nearly all their land, and frequent starvation. Some whites hunted Indians for sport and rounded up children and sold them.

It was not until the 1920s that the situation improved markedly. In 1928, after the federal government declared Indians to be citizens of the United States, California passed the California Indian Jurisdictional Act, which, as the forerunner of the legislation that brought the U.S. Indian Claims

Commission into existence, enabled Indians of California to sue the federal government for damages suffered as a result of loss of land and resources. This led to a slow but steady assumption of responsibility by both state and federal government until 1954, when the U.S. Congress voted to withdraw from any responsibilities to Indians. In 1958 the United States began a slow withdrawal by giving land titles to all California Indians who asked for them. Legal complexities developed, but the process continued into the 1970s.

By 1960 there were 117 reservations and rancherias in California that belonged to Indians under trust arrangement with the federal government. Twenty-eight of these are reservations created at different times since the 1850s, most being very small, the largest consisting of 87,000 acres in the Hoopa Valley in the northwestern part of the state. The rancherias are sometimes less than an acre and usually are the sites of houses that Indians had occupied from the mission period. The residents of the rancherias often have little sense of identity as Indians but consider themselves ethnically distinct from both Anglos and Mexican Americans, which they express in terms of locality.

Luiseños

From San Diego north to Santa Barbara, Franciscan missionaries with Spanish troops established five mission settlements, which gave their names to coastal-dwelling Indians —Diegueño, Luiseño, Juaneño, Gabrielino, and Fernandeño. These Indians and another group culturally similar to them to their north—the Chumash—numbered possibly as many as 25,000 when the first missions were established in 1769. By 1960 this population had been reduced to about 2,000, the largest being the Luiseño, with 1,200–1,300. No communities of Fernandeños, Gabrielinos, or Juaneños have been recorded, but individuals scattered through the highly urbanized region of coastal southern California still identify themselves in those terms.

The Luiseños, like the other Mission Indians, were first recruited on a voluntary basis by the Spanish missionaries. They built the mission of San Luis Rey, a massive stone building, and worked the large acreage surrounding it, doing all the manual labor to establish orchards, vineyards, and fields for wheat, corn, and a variety of other crops. The Luiseño territory included not only a strip on the coast but also an extensive inland area for hunting and gathering. At first their work at the mission establishment was seasonal, but very soon they were forced to remain permanently, send their children to school at the mission, and abide by a rigid schedule of workdays. Men and women lived separately in dormitories, which became more and more crowded. The simply organized Luiseño communities largely broke down as the people were forced to live under missionary rule. Cultural assimilation was rapid, and language and traditions were lost. By the time of the Mexican War for independence in the 1820s, most Luiseños lived under Spanish rule, although a few small communities still existed inland from the mission.

In 1834, under Mexican rule, the management of the missions was taken from the priests. The Indian workers were dismissed, and the land was taken over by politicians and landlords. Serrano and other Indians of the interior raided the Mexican settlements. The Luiseños scattered, some joining the inland Cahuillas, others moving to Los Angeles or wherever they could get work. Many Diegueños also moved from the south to Los Angeles. The coastal communities were broken up, and Spanish replaced the Indian languages.

Poverty-stricken Indians were paid the lowest possible wages. Drunken at payday, many were herded into open corrals and their labor sold on Monday mornings to the highest bidder. Some built huts near the old missions or on parts of their former territories and fell under the rule of other Indians who were recognized as captains, who acted as go-betweens with white employers. Under these circumstances the Gabrielinos, Fernandeños, and Juaneños disappeared from white notice, but some communities of Diegüeños and Luiseños survived into the 20th century and began to receive some state and federal aid and land protection. An unorganized group of 87 Chumash survived as separate families in a rancheria near their former mission. Most of the 28 reservations placed under trust during the 20th century are in southern California in the former mission back country, where the Luiseños now live.

Cahuillas

In the 1970s some Cahuilla Indians possessed one of the most valuable reservations in the United States. Partially located in Palm Springs, where land values have risen tremendously, the Palm Springs Reservation houses 96 residents. Other Cahuillas lived on four small reservations in the surrounding mountains. The total Cahuilla population is about 530, about 2,000 fewer than in the 18th century, when they roamed over the San Jacinto Mountains and the desert north of Imperial Valley.

The affairs of the Palm Springs Reservation are managed by a tribal council, which during the 1950s was composed of five women. The Cahuillas are completely assimilated culturally, living like other well-to-do citizens of Palm Springs. Their cohesion as a group rests entirely on their kinship relations and their common interest in the valuable land, the management of which they are negotiating with the BIA.

The Cahuillas, like the coastal mission Indians, speak a Shoshonean (Uto-Aztecan) language. At the time of first contact with Europeans, they had adapted to the extremely arid conditions of the Coachella Valley and vicinity, living in small clusters of brush shelters around deep hand-dug wells. Mesquite beans were their major source of subsistence, or if they lived higher up in the mountains, acorns. They hunted and gathered seeds and were the only Indians of southern California to make pottery. In other respects their culture and social organization matched the simplicity of other tribes.

Cahuillas were not involved in the mission system of

forced labor. They were generally friendly with Anglo-Americans and acted as a bulwark against raiding tribes from farther east. One of their headmen, Juan Antonio, was well known during the late 19th century and much relied on by whites for assistance. After the secularization of the missions, the Cahuillas sheltered Luiseños, Diegueños, and other Indians.

Like many other California peoples, they negotiated a treaty with the government in 1852, which guaranteed the areas later to become their reservations. However, this treaty was never ratified, and during the 75 years after 1852 they steadily lost land to encroaching whites. Moreover, neither the state nor the federal government assumed any active responsibility for aiding them. As their situation deteriorated, the writer Helen Hunt Jackson (1830–1885) was asked by the Interior Department to make a report on the condition of southern California Indians preparatory to providing some kind of assistance. When her report was ignored, she decided to write a novel to draw attention to what she regarded as inexcusable neglect. She chose as her subject a Cahuilla woman known as Ramona and named the novel for her. It became a best seller and probably influenced the passage of the Mission Indian Relief Act by the California legislature. The act resulted in no immediate aid for California Indians, but by 1962 portions of the old Cahuilla territory were put in trust status and thus the valuable Palm Springs land stayed in Cahuilla hands. The Cahuillas never organized under the provisions of the IRA but did develop an effective tribal council.

Pomos

In northern California, Indians did not have early intensive contacts with Europeans. It was not until the middle of the 19th century, when Anglo-Americans discovered gold in their territory and began to arrive by the thousands, that contacts began. A group that is typical of the Indians of central and northern California is the Pomos, who live in a deep, mountain-ringed valley near Ukiah. There were 900 Pomos in the 1960s, a reduction of perhaps 10,000 from their number in the 17th century. They are intermixed with whites, other Indians, and Filipinos, so it is not possible to identify a Pomo as Indian unless his or her family connections are known. Their houses and clothing are like those of their neighbors. They belong to Mormon and Pentecostal churches and work in a variety of occupations. Other Pomos live in cities, where they hold many different types of jobs. There is a Pomo Tribal Council, organized under the IRA in the 1940s. Pomo crafts, especially baskets, are well known for their fine quality and are sold at intertribal functions and in craft stores throughout the United States. There has been a revival of interest in their native ceremonial dances during the 1960s.

The Pomos and their neighbors in Ukiah have not always been on good terms. In their early contacts with Spaniards, some Pomos were captured for the slave trade, but relatively few. Small-scale clashes occurred with early Anglo-American miners crossing or prospecting in their country, but there was never any organized warfare by the Pomos. They lived like most native Californians in small villages that were not organized politically beyond the local community and not at all for war. They lived by gathering acorns and horse chestnuts and by hunting game. Their first extended contacts with white men were with settlers taking up land for cattle and sheep raising. When white women joined these men, they immediately cut off intimate contacts with Indians; they refused to hire Pomo women as servants and generally established a segregated community. Their land having been appropriated, the Indians were squeezed out of town and into migratory labor, picking fruit and hops. It was from contacts with other migrant workers rather than from the people of segregated Ukiah that they learned white ways.

By 1939 the Pomos began to take action against the segregation and discriminatory employment practices in the town of Ukiah. The women organized a Pomo Mothers' Club, which sponsored craft shows and made fine baskets. They held intertribal dances and revived the elaborate dance costumes of earlier days. They hired a lawyer who successfully combated segregation, so that by 1946 the Pomos were living on an equal basis with other residents.

Other Indians living in California are the Bear Rivers, Chemehuevis, Fort Mohaves, Hupas, Karoks, Katos, Kawaiisus, Maidus, Miwoks, Monos, Paiutes, Pit Rivers, Shastas, Shoshones, Tolowas, Tübatulabal, Tule Rivers, Vanyumes, Wappos, Washoes, Wintuns, Wiyots, Yokuts, and Yuroks

THE NORTHWEST

In 1960 there were approximately 28,000 Indians in Oregon and Washington, about one-quarter of the population at the time of initial contact with Europeans. The great decrease in population was a result of many factors, including introduced diseases, forced change in their ways of life, and absorption into the general population, all under largely peaceful conditions. The reduction in the number of distinct ethnic groups was also fairly substantial. About 1960 there were 40 groups; at the beginning of contact there were 55 or more. The figures on numbers of groups, however, even more than in other regions, should be taken as only suggestive. The nature of ethnic identification before contact remains largely unknown, but it does appear that ethnic boundaries between groups remained rather indistinct.

The placement of several different groups on a single reservation, with consequent important influences on Indian identity patterns, is one of the distinguishing characteristics of the region, especially in eastern Oregon. Groups that had been separate before reservation days merged. The former

Klamath reservation included not only Klamaths but also Modocs, Paiutes, and others. The Colville Reservation of northeastern Washington was set aside expressly for groups that had no treaty arrangements with the federal government: some 14 tribes are represented by small bands, some consisting of only a few families. The Warm Springs Reservation in northern Oregon has some ten different tribes represented.

In western Washington the various Salish- and Nootkan-speaking peoples, numerous but all small in population, were placed on small reservations within their former hunting and fishing territories; in contrast with many tribes farther east, they were not moved about repeatedly.

During the 1960s the Indians of western Washington became especially interested in the assertion of fishing rights along the rivers, inlets, and coasts where they had traditionally lived, and they initiated numerous lawsuits to reestablish these rights, claiming they had not specifically been taken away by the numerous land treaties. In general, as key cases came to court, the Indian rights were affirmed, and rivers that white commercial and sports fishermen had been exploiting came again under partial control of the Indians, some of whom were on reservations that no longer included fishing areas.

Klamaths

The largest Indian group in Oregon during the 1960s was the Klamaths, with a population reported as 1,717. The Klamaths had a reservation until 1955, but the federal government withdrew from its trust relationship over the land in 1954, and the Klamath Tribal Council, which had been organized under the provisions of the IRA, was disbanded. These actions were a result of the policy known as termination, eliminating all special relationships between the Klamaths and the federal government. More than 70 percent of the members of the tribal body had voted for withdrawal of federal trust over the reservation land, with the understanding that the government would buy the extensive timberland owned in common by the tribe, make it into a national forest, and distribute per capita payments of $43,500 to the tribe's members. However, by the late 1960s only about 570 of the former tribal members had been judged competent, had received the per capita payments, and thus severed ties with the federal government. Approximately 250 of these continued to live on what had been the reservation.

Of the other 1,200 or so, the great majority were judged by the federal government as not fully competent to manage their own affairs and were continued under protective management. Thus, for only about one-third of the tribe there was new status as wholly independent United States citizens; for the great majority this had not taken place. For them the most decisive element in the new situation was the destruction of the tribal political structure. They chose an executive committee from among their ranks to handle business matters with the bank, but other than that their political life had merged with non-Indians.

As many Klamaths live outside the former reservation area as on it. They are scattered through the immediate rural area, in Klamath Falls, and in other towns and cities of Oregon and the West Coast. Most are members of Methodist or Four Square Gospel congregations. The Klamath language is spoken in very few homes, although it is frequently used in public meetings and has been, as much as English, the language of the tribal council. Klamaths are businessmen, cattlemen, farmers, and wage workers in a wide range of the regional occupations.

The 1,200–2,000 Klamaths aboriginally were of the Plateau culture, hunting and gathering, living in earth lodges in small villages, with no political organization beyond the local community, except sporadically for war-making. Penutian-language speakers, they had some contacts with Plains Indians. They ranged over southeastern and central Oregon and were associated with the Modocs to their southwest.

They did not obtain horses and firearms until the 1820s. It was not until the 1840s that they began to figure in white history, first as raiders of the Pit River Indians and later, after a serious epidemic had reduced their numbers to a few hundred, as providers and guides for the expeditions led by John Charles Frémont in the 1840s. For the most part they avoided warfare with whites, and after 1859 a peace party headed by a prominent headman named Lileks fairly consistently sought peace, even though white encroachments often gave rise also to hostile leadership. A treaty signed by Klamath leaders in 1864 resulted in establishment of a reservation in 1870 and an agency; a farmer was assigned to teach them.

The Klamaths adapted rapidly and easily to new ways, abandoning their hunting and gathering economy for farming, stock raising, and logging. They accepted the administrative structure of the agency and the leadership of a strong superintendent, who managed the tribal police and courts. Even forced reduction in the activity of shamans was accepted, and many joined the Methodist church. Nevertheless, the Ghost Dance religion took hold for a short time, and aspects of native religion continue in the form of the Earth Lodge cult and the Dream Dance.

Allotment of land began in 1895 and was completed in 1910, but it resulted not in opening the reservation to white settlement, but rather in tribal ownership of the reservation's valuable timber resources. The timber was harvested under BIA management, and by 1950 every Klamath (along with Modocs and Paiutes) was receiving an annual payment of $800, which kept many from taking up regular employment. For others the income provided economic security as they raised cattle, farmed, or worked off the reservation. The Klamath tribal council, organized in 1908, clashed with the BIA superintendent regarding the basis for tribal membership; the superintendent favored membership according to percentage of Klamath Indian descent, while the Indian leadership favored membership according to degree of participation in reservation community life. Bitter factionalism developed in tribal council affairs and characterized Klamath life until the council was dissolved in 1955. Different constitutions were adopted, the last in 1950. Shortly after the disbanding of the tribal council, the Klamaths joined the National Congress of American Indians and became very active in pan-Indian activities.

Planning for individual distribution of the tribal resources began in 1910, and over the years various plans were presented and became the focus of political conflicts. Seldon Kirk, active in the Committee for the Perpetuation of the Tribe, led the faction for maintenance of the tribe in some form. During the early 1950s the two major factions agreed on formation of a tribal corporation as the means for eliminating government supervision, but Congress implemented its plan for termination, although tribal members generally had a very inadequate understanding of the alternatives.

Wascos

The two largest among the ten Indian groups on the Warm Springs Reservation (now the largest reservation in Oregon) are the Sahaptin-speaking Warm Springs people and the Chinookan-speaking Wascos. There were about 500 Wascos during the 1960s. The Wascos are much mixed genetically with the Chinookan-speaking Wishrams, who live on the Yakima Reservation in Washington, some other Indians, and whites; most Wascos, in fact, are married to non-Wascos. The Wascos are nearly surrounded by peoples of the Plateau-type culture (Yakimas, Klikitats, Teninos) and live in scattered camps with no overall tribal organization. The Indian language most Wasco children learn on the reservation is the Sahaptin of the Warm Springs tribe.

In most respects the Wascos are much more assimilated culturally than the other Indians of the reservation; their houses, clothing, and occupations are like those of whites.

They raise some cattle and horses, and a few farm. They depend considerably on income from the sale of timber, cattle, and grain produced on the reservation. Until 1950, when a dam was built on the Columbia River, they fished seasonally for salmon, which is typical of the Chinookan culture. In 1938 the Indians of the reservation joined to form an IRA-type tribal council, in which the Wascos held the most offices and took the most vigorous interest. The tribal council was very successful in developing income-producing business enterprises with the aid of expert professional advice. Wascos are members of the Presbyterian and Indian Shaker churches, but most also participate in the Indian Longhouse religion. Occasionally they stage a complex traditional ceremony called the Wasco Dance, but there is more interest in rodeos and various traditional gambling games. The Plains craft of beadwork on buckskin is prominent among the women.

The Wascos and other Chinookans—in contrast with Sahaptin-speakers—responded peacefully to white pressures, readily signing treaties for removal to reservations beginning in 1855. By 1858 the Wascos had moved to the Warm Springs Reservation and immediately began farming and spreading out in individual homesteads. They even gave up their fishing rights with no conflict in 1865. They maintained their concept of a stratified society, including a lowest stratum of slaves, until the 1870s. Traces of the concept survived into the 20th century.

Makahs

In the 1960s there were between 500 and 600 Makah Indians in Washington, most of whom live on a reservation that includes the town of Neah Bay near the tip of Cape Flattery. The Makah occupy the same coastal territory they have lived in since the birth of their traditions. They are in most respects like the whites who live within the reservation area, which includes not only the coastal strip but also a large timber acreage to the south. Makah houses, dress, and occupations are like those of the surrounding peoples; they fish for salmon and halibut, work in the logging industry on their reservation and in other forms of wage work, and provide services for tourists who visit the reservation. They also receive some income from timber sales on land allotted to tribal members. Their tribal council, organized in 1936 and chartered by the federal government a year later, maintains a tribal fund from sales of timber from reservation land held under tribal title.

The Makahs are either bilingual in English and their Nootkan language or speak only English. Many are multilingual in the various Indian languages of the region, like Quinault and Quileute. They are genetically mixed and not readily distinguishable physically from other residents of the region.

A majority are members of the Presbyterian or Apostolic church, and a few belong to the Indian Shaker church. Many call themselves heathens and practice traditional rituals connected with supernatural power-seeking and the spirits of the dead. The Makahs make use of Plains Indian headdresses and other pan-Indian elements of costume in secular ceremonial dances and participate in such dances with other Indians in Washington and elsewhere.

The traditional Makah way of life has been replaced in most of its fundamentals as well as in particular customs, although they have never been relocated from their homeland. Their present area of concentration around Neah Bay is the holy land of their legends, their mythical place of origin, and continues to have much of that meaning for them. Their subsistence still rests heavily on the traditional fishing, although they use mostly new techniques, despite the fact that the fishing banks have been seriously depleted.

The Makahs were one of many Nootkan-speaking groups who lived along the North Pacific coast when whites first arrived. Like the others of the region, they lived in autonomous villages with no tribal organization above the local level. The large plank houses were shared by many family groups. The society was stratified, consisting of a chiefly, or titled, class and a commoner class, as well as a slave class. They practiced the potlatch, a ceremonial feast in which social status was displayed by giving away possessions.

In the course of contact with whites they experienced no important dislocation or large-scale infiltration and invasion, probably because of their location. They ceded to the United States their property rights in a treaty of 1863 and were given a reservation that remained nearly intact for more than a hundred years. They were never put on rations and suffered no conflicts with white settlers.

However, from 1863 until the 1930s aggressive Indian agents dominated their life on the reservation, vigorously pursuing the general BIA assimilation policy. The potlatch, major religious ceremonials, and traditional gambling games were prohibited. The communal houses were torn down and American-style frame houses put up. Long hair was cut and native clothing was replaced forcibly by "citizens' dress." Women were jailed for keeping their houses in a condition the agent regarded as unclean. The agent attempted to force the men to farm, apparently not regarding commercial fishing as a proper economic pursuit for development. From 1874 the children were required to go to boarding schools, where the Makah language was prohibited and Christian religious instruction was required.

The result of these measures during a hundred years was fairly complete cultural replacement and a definite alienation from whites. A strong self-identification as Makahs resulted and, during the 20th century, a broader identification with other Indians in the United States and Canada. This was intensified especially during World War II, when a few white civic leaders attempted to segregate the women's Red Cross groups. The Makahs' continued exclusive possession of their land as a reservation, the resources of which they manage partly through their tribal council, also contributes to the separate identification as Indians. They have learned to shield their concept of social stratification, as well as certain religious practices, from white interference.

Puyallups

Among the many Salish-speaking groups living along the coast of Puget Sound and its tributaries in Washington are the Puyallups. In 1960, 354 Puyallups were living on a reservation in the immediate vicinity of Tacoma. The reservation, however, was in uncertain status and by 1970 was not listed as a reservation by the BIA. As many as 20 families now live on what had been that reservation. Some have small farms; others, including some lawyers and businessmen, work in the city; most are clerical or wage workers. The majority of Puyallups are scattered and separate from one another in northwestern Washington, and a number of families live on Warm Springs Reservation in Oregon. They are culturally indistinguishable from other ethnic groups of the region, and none seem to know anything of the Salish language, which they had formerly spoken.

One group of Puyallups insists that it constitutes an organized tribal group; it maintains a representative tribal council that has made a claim against the U.S. government for the former reservation land. The legal status of this land has been in question for some time, and the legal existence of the tribal council depends on whether the land belongs to the Puyallups. Although the scattered Puyallups maintain no common community or religious life, the land case has increased their awareness of their history.

The Puyallups traditionally ranged along the southern margin of Puget Sound and its tributary, the Puyallup River. Their first contacts with whites came in 1792, but intensive contacts did not begin until 1832, when the Hudson's Bay Company built a post among the Nisqually Indians immediately west of Puyallup territory. The purpose of the post was to oversee the settlement of farm homesteads for Hudson's

Bay Company retirees in the prairie land over which Puyallups and Nisquallies ranged. As settlement spread, there was some resistance by the Indians, but it was quickly controlled, and a treaty was prepared.

The Treaty of Medicine Creek in 1854 was a major turning point in Puyallup life. All the Indians of the southern Puget Sound area ceded their territories and agreed to the creation of three reservations—for Nisquallies, Squaksons, and Puyallups—on Squaxin Island. The Puyallups and others refused to go there, and after a short war the reservation was enlarged, and the Puyallups settled on their portion of the island.

For 30 years relations between Indians and whites in the region were amicable. Many white men married Indian women, and there were many mixed households. There had been no organized tribal life, so the whites made no aggressive efforts to reorganize Indian society, nor did Presbyterian and Catholic missionaries push to replace the Indian religion. The traditional ways of fishing were maintained, and both Indians and whites used the Chinook jargon for communication. By 1874, however, the Bureau of Indian Affairs broke up the communal dwellings and made allotments to individuals, which were inalienable and could not be sold. By this time there had been a great deal of cultural assimilation: nearly all Puyallups spoke some English and dressed and lived largely like whites. They continued to be self-supporting in very much their old patterns of work.

When Tacoma began to be important as a major railroad terminus in the mid-1880s, railroad companies tried to put a major line through the reservation. The Puyallups resisted, but after litigation and Congressional intervention, the allotments needed by the railroad were sold and tracks were built across the reservation. The immediate result of the conflict was increased disorganization in Puyallup society and the murder of individuals who had attempted to provide leadership. More allotments were sold, and Puyallup society became steadily more disorganized. During the 20th century it ceased to exist as an organized unit. It was only with the passage of the IRA in 1934 that new efforts were made to vitalize the tribe. Land was secured for a reservation, but its legality remained questionable, and the struggle over it continued into the 1970s.

Other Indians living in the Northwest in the 1970s were the Coast Salish—including the Chehalis, Clallams, Lummis, Nooksacks. Quileutes, Quinaults, Skagits, Skokomishes, Swinomishes, and Tulalips; other tribes were the Cayuses, Chetcos, Colvilles (Salish), Coos Bays, Cowlitzes, Kalispels, Klickitats, Siletzes, Siuslaws, Spokans, Teninos, Umatillas, Upper Umpquas, Walla Wallas, Warm Springs, Weacos, and Yakimas.

ALASKA

The Indian population in Alaska in the 1960s was about 16,000 and was about evenly divided between coastal dwellers, chiefly Tlingits, and interior Athapaskan-speaking peoples, such as the Tananas, the Kutchins, and the Koyukons. Although there are no estimates for all the interior peoples at the time of first European contacts, there is little reason to believe that the Indian population for the whole of Alaska in the 1960s was substantially different from what it was at the beginning of contact. The Indians are, of course, to be distinguished from the other Alaskan natives, the Eskimos and the Aleuts, whose population in the 1960s was twice that of the Indians.

The experience of the Alaskan Indians since first contact differed in very important respects from that of all other Indians of the United States. For example, there was practically no warfare between whites and Indians; no treaties were made between the United States or Russian government and the Indian tribes; neither government assumed the kind of close control over Indian lives that took place in all other parts of the United States; and there were no reservations. It is also notable that there was no change in the number of distinct Indian ethnic groups from the beginning of contact until the 1970s.

The Alaskan Indians' early contacts were with Russians, whose government made no legal distinctions between Indians and Russians, although missionaries of the Russian Orthodox church were sent to make converts. When the United States bought Alaska in 1867, it assumed no responsibility for what were designated in the treaty of cession as the "uncivilized tribes," who did not live in the Russian settlements. Thus, there was no special relationship between the Alaskan Indians and the government until the passage of the IRA in 1934. A 1936 amendment to that act defined Indian political status in terms of village rights to manage land in common and also opened the way for villages to become reservations, but the villages were generally distrustful of the government and did not ask for reservation status. During the 1940s and 1950s business interests in Alaska repeatedly sought to extinguish all Indian and Eskimo rights to land, a matter that was not settled until 1971, when 40 million acres were declared in native possession, and compensation for other lands acquired by whites was set at $500 million, plus royalties from oil income. The administration of the native lands was placed in the hands of an all-native board of management.

Tlingits

In the 1960s the Tlingits lived in some 25 locations along the Pacific Coast and coastal islands from Yakutat Bay to Ketchikan in the southeastern extension of Alaska. Several of these sites are identical to those where they lived before European contact. Apparently the Tlingits have inhabited the area for several millennia, although some of their traditions come from the south and the east. Tlingits also occupy former white settlements that whites abandoned after the gold rush of the 1890s. Still others live scattered in Juneau, Anchorage, and other coastal towns. They work in the fish canneries, at various kinds of wage work, and in traditional subsistence fishing and hunting. Most are Presbyterians, Roman Catholics, Anglicans, or Salvation Army members, and traditional ceremonies are carried out only for secular celebrations or for the benefit of tourists. Most speak English, only a few retaining any use of the Tlingit language, which belongs to the Nadene linguistic family. Clothes and houses are like those of neighboring whites.

Most Tlingit villages have chapters of the Alaska Native Brotherhood and the Alaska Native Sisterhood, affiliates of the Tlingit tribewide organization, which was set up in 1912 by two Presbyterian converts. Strongly advocating full cultural assimilation, including the replacement of the Tlingit language with English, the organization played an important role in securing voting rights, which were denied Indians and Eskimos until 1922, and has been quite effective in combating the segregation and widespread discrimination that have characterized white–Indian relationships since the late 19th century. After the territorial government passed the Jurisdictional Claims Act in 1935, the organization began to push land and other claims and in 1971 secured recognition of native rights to the land and its resources. In 1966 the brotherhood expanded to include Eskimos and Athapaskan Indians and became the nucleus of the Alaska Federation of Natives.

The Tlingits were a maritime people who lived by fishing and by hunting sea mammals and forest game when Russians first made contact with them in 1741. Their culture was one of the most complex ever evolved by a nonagricultural people, but they did not have tribal government or other large-scale organization. The village, or the clan within the village, was the highest unit of loyalty and cooperation, except occasionally during time of war.

Although the Tlingits traded furs with the Russians, they kept their villages clear of any political domination, demonstrating a readiness to fight off any encroachments. They successfully blockaded extension of the fur trade to inland Athapaskan peoples during the late 19th century. They accepted a Russian Orthodox priest, but few converts were made. Later in 1877, after the U.S. purchase of Alaska, Presbyterians came, set up schools, and were active in conversion. Their influence resulted in much cultural replacement and a strong tendency toward assimilation. They opposed cremation, multiple wives, the custom of maintaining slaves, the practices of shamans, and the potlatch, which was highly important in the Tlingit social system. The potlatch and the use of totem poles, which were significant in Tlingit culture, were eliminated by about 1904. Since the 1960s there has been a considerable revival of traditional arts, including the carving of totem poles, which Tlingits continue to use in their social ranking system, rather than for purchase by tourists or museums.

Athapaskans

Very different from the coastal Tlingits, the seven groups of Athapaskan speakers live in inland Alaska. Although they were never removed from their land and continue to use their traditional hunting territories, profound changes have occurred. Once hunters and fishermen living in simply organized nomadic bands, they ceased to be nomadic in the course of contacts with Europeans and were concentrated into more or less stabilized villages of as many as 600 inhabitants. In the 1960s there were between 50 and 60 villages, each separate in its organization. While they continue to speak the seven different languages they used at the time of contact, there are some English-speakers in every village, especially since the 1930s, when the U.S. government began to build village schools. Nearly all have become Christians, either Roman Catholic or Presbyterian.

The Athapaskans still trap much as they did in the late 1700s, when the Russians and the English vigorously brought them into the fur trade. However, because of the depletion of fur-bearing animals, a steep decline in fur prices, and their own inclination to remain close to the stores, schools, baseball diamonds, and nursing stations in their villages, trapping has assumed a steadily more minor role in their lives. They support themselves chiefly by wage work for BIA or U.S. Army installations, logging, or other sources and through government welfare. They remain isolated, seeing few whites in their relatively remote villages, but a few have been active in the expanded Alaska Federation of Natives.

URBAN INDIANS

In 1970 the United States Census listed the total Indian population of the United States at 791,839. Of this total, 340,367 —about 43 percent—were listed as urban, that is, living in cities and towns. About one-fourth of the total Indian population—192,316—lived in cities of 100,000 or more. Most projections indicated that by 1980 more than half the Indian population would be urban.

The increase in urban-dwelling Indians was quite different from that of U.S. city dwellers in general. There was no steady increment in the urban Indian population through the late 19th and early 20th centuries, corresponding to the growing urbanization of the population as a whole. On the contrary, the Indians were almost exclusively a rural population until the 1890s, when they began slowly to join in the mainstream movement to the cities. The urban movement was not marked until the 1940s, and the greatest increase has taken place since 1950.

The factors resulting in the urbanization, or lack of it, of Indians also were notably different from those of the general population. First of all, government policies of removing whole tribes westward and concentrating them on reservations increased their segregation. Except for a few remnants of the peoples of the northeastern states who were absorbed into towns in Massachusetts, Rhode Island, Connecticut, and New York, Indians continued to live in separate communities from whites through the first three-quarters of the 19th century. Here and there individual Iroquois and others found their way into the growing towns of the East, such as Albany and New York, but these few (who often were strikingly successful in the white man's world, such as Ely S. Parker, who became a commissioner of Indian affairs) were rarities.

The appreciable movement of Indians into towns after 1890 is also related to the General Allotment Act of 1887. The 30-year period following the passage of the act was one of profound upheaval for most Indians. Tens of thousands suddenly became landless people, as the newly allotted acres slipped out of their grasp. Whites acquired land on what had been reservations, moved in, and established towns in the midst of the disrupted Indian communities. Indians found their only means of subsistence either in the white towns near the reservations or farther away in the cities. The process of moving into more urban ways of life, usually as wage workers, was aided to some extent by the boarding-school program of the BIA. Small numbers of young people in the boarding schools, as at Riverside, Calif., Albuquerque, N.Mex., Phoenix, Ariz., and Chilocco, Okla., took jobs as domestics or in other capacities in those cities where the schools were located and, at least for a time, stayed away from their homes in Indian country. A few settled permanently in these cities or nearby. Some accepted jobs in the Wild West Shows of the period and traveled widely, often settling permanently in larger cities, like New York or Los Angeles.

By the 1920s perhaps several thousand Indians lived in towns near reservations and in half a dozen large cities throughout the country. Although the number of Indians who began to live off reservations in this period is not known, it seems probable that there were relatively very few compared with the total Indian population. They were for the most part poor and working in unskilled occupations. The Meriam Report published in 1928 pointed them out as a serious problem for which the BIA was not taking adequate responsibility. Most of the off-reservation Indians lived in what the report called colonies, that is, in small clusters. They uniformly reported that they had left the reservations because of lack of work there and criticized the BIA for having leased land on reservations to whites, who did not provide Indians with jobs.

During the 1930s the numbers of town- and city-dwelling Indians declined, and the population of the reservations increased. The reasons for the return to the reservations were the growing scarcity of jobs in the cities because of the Depression and an increase in jobs on the reservations under the administration of Commissioner John Collier. This was the New Deal period in American political life, and many public works programs on and near reservations were undertaken, the most notable, with respect to influence on Indian life, being those carried out by the Civilian Conservation Corps (CCC). Hundreds of Indians were taken into the corps and employed in a wide variety of jobs, ranging from construction of small check dams for erosion control to extensive water storage and irrigation projects. As a result of these latter projects, many reservations underwent new agricultural development, and the various conservation measures salvaged and improved large range areas. The CCC, which had a special Indian division, may be regarded as the first effort on the part of the government to bring Indians systematically into the national work force on a par with other Americans. A generation of young Indians gained the experience of regular work at standard wages both on and off the reservation. The Depression years resulted, on many reservations, in economic stabilization for Indian families whose lives had been disrupted by land loss and unsuccessful adjustment to white town life. Many individuals gained new abilities to cope with the white man's economic ways.

World War II also helped create a sizable new urban Indian population. During the war some 25,000 Indians volunteered or were drafted into the armed services, where they learned to use English, as few had been forced to previously. A team of Navajo servicemen made a distinguished record in Army Intelligence by using their own language in lieu of code, which enemy code experts found unbreakable. Another 40,000 Indians were estimated to have left reservations for work in war industries, chiefly in West Coast cities. By the end of World War II there were nearly 80,000 urban-dwelling Indians.

Although many Indians returned to reservations when the war ended, the BIA made a special effort to encourage movement to the cities. Lack of employment opportunities and poor social environment on the reservations were given as reasons for the new program, which began at about the same time Congress was preparing legislation to terminate the special relationship between Indian tribes and the federal government. To spearhead the program, Dillon S. Myer was appointed commissioner of Indian affairs in 1948. During the war he had been director of the War Relocation Authority program for resettling the 110,000 Japanese Americans who had been evacuated from their homes and placed in relocation centers; before the end of the war the authority had found jobs for about one-fourth. Myer's achievement in directing this relocation and a multifaceted program for reintegrating evacuees promptly into American life led to his appointment as commissioner.

Modeling policy to some extent on the earlier resettlement program, Myer and his associates established a Relocation Division of the BIA to stimulate movement from the reservations into American cities. The new effort was named the Employment Assistance Program in order to avoid the implication that it was attempting to liquidate the bureau and force all Indians off the reservations. The program became the major influence in the large migration of Indians to the cities during the 1950s and 1960s.

Through offices established in Chicago, San Francisco, Los Angeles, Denver, Minneapolis, and other large cities, the BIA assisted Indians who left the reservation in finding employment, housing, welfare aid, and other services. By 1968 the bureau reported that it had assisted at least 50,000 individuals to settle in major cities, chiefly in Los Angeles, San Francisco–Oakland, and Chicago, although it was also reported that some 35 percent of those relocated during the 1960s returned to reservations. There is no doubt that the BIA relocation program was a major influence in the sudden new shift from an almost exclusively rural population to a high proportion of urban residents.

By 1970 the largest concentrations of urban Indians were in the following states:

California	60,000–65,000
Oklahoma	27,000–32,000
Arizona	18,000–20,000
Minnesota	10,000–15,000
Illinois	10,000–12,000
Washington	9,000–9,500
Texas	8,000–8,500
New Mexico	5,000–6,000
Michigan	5,000–6,000
Wisconsin	4,000–4,500
Oregon	4,000–4,500
Massachusetts	3,500–4,000
Arkansas	3,500–3,800
Pennsylvania	3,000–3,600

The cities with the largest Indian populations were the following:

Los Angeles	47,000
San Francisco–Oakland	18,000
Tulsa, Okla.	15,000
Minneapolis–St. Paul	13,000
Oklahoma City	12,000
Chicago	12,000
Phoenix, Ariz.	10,000

Urbanization of American Indians was also taking place in cities and towns close to reservations, especially near the largest ones, and it was apparent that different processes were at work in these locales. In some areas, such as western New York State, New Mexico, and the Dakotas, this kind of urbanization had been going on for many years prior to World War II, and it increased and intensified after the war. With the tremendous growth in the Navajo population during the 20th century, the reservation population spilled over into towns like Gallup and Farmington, N.Mex., and within the reservation, urban concentrations developed around Shiprock and Window Rock. Rapid City in the Black Hills country of South Dakota attracted Sioux from the nearby Pine Ridge and Rosebud reservations. Similarly, the urbanization of the Salish-, Sahaptin-, and Chinookan-speaking peoples of western Washington began early as Seattle and Tacoma expanded. Buffalo, N.Y., and other cities in the vicinity of the Seneca and other Iroquois reservations became the residence of Iroquois families early in the 19th century. However, the processes by which Indians moved into cities near the reservations differed substantially from those in the largest United States cities, the most important way being an intensification of Indian identity in the large cities, which was not usually apparent in the towns near reservations.

The experience of some urban enclaves, founded by Indians long before the BIA began relocation efforts, illustrates this point. For example, in 1970 there were 800 Mohawks in the North Gowanus section of Brooklyn, N.Y., who had lived there since the 1920s. They had come in response to a demand for their skills as high steel workers on bridges and skyscrapers, such as Rockefeller Center in New York City. The Brooklyn enclave constituted a well-defined neighborhood served by a Presbyterian church where the minister preached in the Mohawk language. Although they have made a satisfactory adaptation to urban life, the Mohawks do not regard the urban settlement as their home. Most remain Catholic, as they were on their home reservation of

Caughnawaga in Quebec; they often send their children to the reservation to be educated, and most spend long summer vacations there, where each family owns land and where most plan to retire. The urban settlement is the scene of only one phase in each family cycle, but it is a stable element in which Mohawk Indian identity receives emphatic expression through the use of the Mohawk language, participation in the Iroquois Longhouse religion, and active interest in various pan-Indian pow-wow activities.

Indians in other large cities, however, do not live in such sharply defined enclaves. In Los Angeles there are groups of Cherokees and Creeks from Oklahoma who first came to the city in the 1930s during the dustbowl migrations from Arkansas and Oklahoma. In Minneapolis, as employment opportunities on the Minnesota and Dakota reservations declined even before the Depression, a small, steady trickle of Indian families established themselves in that city. These Indian migrants, unlike the Mohawks, had no distinctive occupational specialties, nor were they able to cluster in the same neighborhood. They nevertheless maintained consciousness of their Indian identity to a greater or lesser degree and were vitalized in this respect during the 1950s and 1960s with the new influx of Indian migrants. This sense of identity emphasizes participation in pan-Indian symbols and activities more than tribal distinctiveness.

Where there are the heaviest concentrations of reservation population, Indians have moved out somewhat beyond the reservation borders into the neighboring towns, where the tendency to lose their cultural distinctiveness and sense of Indian identity seems stronger than in the large cities. Certain segments of such groups, however, seem to develop a capacity for behaving acceptably in both Indian and non-Indian cultures.

Rapid City, S.Dak., one near-reservation community, is an example of this phenomenon. Some Sioux families have lived there since before World War II and have become strongly oriented toward middle-class white ways. They live like their non-Indian neighbors and are concerned with getting ahead economically and rising in the class system. They identify with Indians only for very special purposes and generally dissociate themselves actively from Indians arriving from reservations. In Rapid City, as elsewhere, there was a large increase in the number of Indians during and after World War II. By 1955 in this town of 50,000, there were 5,000 Sioux, and their numbers have continued to grow. The new arrivals are usually desperately seeking work, often remain unemployed, and speak both substandard English and substandard Dakota. For the most part, they live in tents and shacks and contrast with the older Indian residents in their adoption of lower-class rather than middle-class ways. The longer-settled Indians pride themselves on being mixed-bloods. A fairly sharp distinction is maintained between the older and the newer Indian migrants. Similar processes of cultural reorientation of earlier Indian migrants are apparent in Albuquerque, Phoenix, and other near-reservation cities, as well as their separation from those who came later, during the 1950s and 1960s.

By 1970, 47,000 Indians lived in Los Angeles County, including members of 101 tribes from all over the United States. Most numerous are Navajos from the Southwest and Sioux from the northern plains; next in numbers are Pueblos from New Mexico and Cherokees, Creeks, and Choctaws from Oklahoma. The list also includes Chickahominies, Mohicans, Potawatomis, Nanticokes, Mandans, Delawares, Iroquois, and Kiowas. Beginning with handfuls of the original displaced natives of the area, such as the Gabrielinos and Diegueños, the Indian population was slightly increased during the late 1800s by other remnants of small California Indian groups dispersed by the new immigrant miners and ranchers. A substantial addition resulted from the dustbowl migrations of the 1930s, chiefly Cherokees, Creeks, Choctaws, and Seminoles from Oklahoma. Some 6,000 of these took up residence in the Los Angeles area during the Depression and constituted, by the 1950s, the major Indian population.

Meanwhile, the industries of World War II had begun to

draw Indians from all over the United States. During the 1950s the majority were from Arizona, New Mexico, the Dakotas, and Montana. As the BIA relocation program came into full operation in the early 1950s, the rapid increase in number of Indians led to a wholly new situation. In the late 1950s as many as 1,300 Indians a year arrived in Los Angeles. The newcomers had no special preparation for urban living, although some had served in the armed forces. All were from reservations where they had been unable to find employment, and none had special skills to offer. Some 86 percent spoke an Indian language and used English imperfectly. Those who succeeded in getting work went into low paying unskilled jobs or service occupations that did not require a good speaking knowledge of English. Eventually 37 percent returned to their reservations. Despite the high rate of failure at adaptation, it must be emphasized that the great majority of those who came stayed, and some moved permanently into jobs and situations that they found satisfactory. The reservation life no longer attracted them, and they became established urban Indians.

The very great majority of the Navajos in Los Angeles are essentially rural people from areas of the reservation where contacts with whites were at a minimum, where urban occupations were unknown, and where the language of daily life was Navajo. Consequently, those who remain in the city through the initial period of difficult adjustment associate with one another rather than with whites or with other Indians. This seems largely true of Pueblos also, even though their background is that of town-dwelling people.

The situation of the next largest group of migrants, from the several Sioux reservations of the Dakotas, contrasted markedly with that of the Navajos. They had experienced much disorganization in their native society largely as a result of the infiltration of whites on their reservations after land allotment. They, therefore, had had some association with whites, and many were a little better prepared as a result of occupational experience in the towns of their region.

They were somewhat better able to use English than the Navajos. These factors have led to a different adjustment pattern from that of the Navajos, and the Sioux are able to associate with persons other than fellow Sioux. This has not led to a loss of their Indian identity, but rather to a wider association with other tribes and to an intensification of pan-Indian identity. This kind of adaptation is also characteristic of many others, such as Kiowas, Iroquois, and Omahas.

Few Indian families in Los Angeles live very close to one another, and Indian neighborhoods have not developed. The most important, or at least most widely attended, organizations are the churches. More Indians are Catholic than any other denomination, and 70 percent attend church more or less regularly, 27 percent being involved in all-Indian congregations. There are nine fundamentalist Protestant churches composed chiefly of Indians, and one Mormon (Latter-day Saints) congregation. The largest Indian church, composed largely of Navajos, is an Assembly of God group.

More is known about Indians in the San Francisco Bay area than about any other urban Indian population. In 1970 the U.S. Census counted about 12,000 concentrated in the vicinity of San Francisco and Oakland and another 4,000 near San Jose. These figures are probably an undercount; it might be safer to assume that there are nearly 20,000 Indians living in this region. Like the movement of Indians into the Los Angeles area, the migration into the San Francisco Bay area tremendously accelerated after the 1940s. Similarly, there are no contiguous-residence Indian neighborhoods, and, as in Los Angeles, 100 tribes are represented.

The Intertribal Friendship House, founded and maintained by the Society of Friends, plays an important role in bringing Indians together. It is managed by a non-Indian board of directors and provides various services for assistance in adapting to city life, such as vocational training and welfare aid. Most important in Indian life, it sponsors social dances, classes of various kinds, and athletic events and provides a meeting place for a ladies' club, a young peoples' club, and a Navajo club, among others.

The Bay Area American Indian Council, managed by an all-Indian board of directors, formed in opposition to Friendship House to bring about more Indian participation in policy making. Its functions are very similar to those of Friendship House, but it also encourages interest in political issues and Indian participation in political activities. Many associations, both formal and informal, meet at the council center, which sponsors both social and ceremonial dance groups. Certain tribes have organized associations among themselves, such as the Navajos, the Pueblos, the Tlingit, the Haida, and the Pomo; other associations focus on pan-Indian activities, with members from many different tribes. They engage actively in pan-Indian dance and music and use pan-Indian symbolism, each tribal group making its own distinctive contribution within this context. Pan-Indian-oriented associations have been formed by the Oklahoma peoples, such as the Cherokees and Creeks, and by the Chippewas from Montana and Minnesota. The intensification of a pan-Indian sense of identity is fostered by these associations.

A third major concentration of urban Indians is in the Chicago area, where much the same patterns obtain as in the California cities: great acceleration in migration during and immediately after World War II, and 90 to 100 tribes in the total population, but with the heaviest representation from Sioux, Chippewa, and Winnebago and other western Great Lakes peoples. In Chicago, however, clubs limited to a single tribe are less important than the pan-Indian associations. As in San Francisco, Indian centers play a prominent role in bringing Indians together, as well as in giving varied assistance in the urban adjustment process. There are two such institutions—the Chicago American Indian Center, managed by an all-Indian board of directors, and the St. Augustine's Center, managed by the Episcopal church. The American Indian Center is an important meeting place for a

variety of organizations, ranging from Boy Scouts and Alco-
holics Anonymous to the Sioux and Winnebago clubs,
which, despite their names, are pan-Indian in orientation.
The movement of Indians into the cities has proceeded on
a quite different basis from the urbanization of European or
Asian immigrants. It is not characterized by the growth of
extensive contiguous neighborhoods in which thousands of
persons of similar cultural backgrounds live in subcultural
enclaves. The urbanization of Indians in the United States
has been a relatively small-scale movement of individuals
and small family groups from quite different tribal cultural
backgrounds. Nevertheless, a sense of common interest and
problems was fostered by the Employment Assistance Program, which applied the common category of Indian to all
the migrants, thereby reinforcing preexisting reservation attitudes. The most characteristic cultural process has been the
stimulation of a sense of pan-Indian identity transcending
tribal identities. The expression of pan-Indianism takes
many forms in athletic clubs, dance groups, and councils
that embrace, or purport to represent, all the Indians of a
given city. Important among these are the strongly politically oriented organizations that arose during the late 1960s,
such as the American Indian Movement, which adopted a
militant program first formulated by the urban Indians of
Minneapolis.

Urban Indian organizations, often actively supported by
Indian students on university campuses, sought to give
leadership to Indians on reservations during the late 1960s
and 1970s, but with little success. While considerable numbers of urban Indians maintain contact with their families on
reservations, close personal relations had not by the mid-
1970s brought about acceptance by reservation Indians of
the politically militant organizations. There developed a division between the reservation leadership generally and the
urban leadership. The leaders of tribal councils on the reservations represent a conservative position, including cooperation with the BIA, and an easy-going leadership, which

had grown up since the 1930s under the conditions of the IRA.

On the other hand, the urban and student leaders view themselves as having much in common with minority groups in the United States generally; they espouse civil rights causes and have been influenced by the viewpoints of blacks and Mexican Americans. Such a conception of themselves was foreign to the reservation residents. Militant movement activities carried to reservations have received either very little support or, most frequently, active opposition. Nevertheless, a new set of ideas about their place in the United States was injected into Indian life as a result of the rise of the urban leadership.

By the 1970s an urban segment of the Indian population had become permanently established. While nearly half of all Indians were listed as residing in urban areas, the number that could be regarded as permanent urban-dwellers was not known; for many, movement between the reservations and the cities was constant. The Indian population of New York City exhibits perhaps the extremes in adaptation: of the 2,000 Indian residents of New York, only the 800 Mohawks maintain strong, definite ties with their reservation. The other 1,200 are largely second-generation city dwellers from 30 to 40 different tribes. Born in New York of parents who for the most part settled there many years earlier, they are permanently established as New Yorkers and have broken their reservation ties. However, they pursue an active interest in Indian traditions and maintain an extremely vigorous organization—the Thunderbird American Indian Dancers—that covers many social and civic functions. In Minneapolis–St. Paul there are also long-established, clearly permanent families who nevertheless have maintained close family relations with reservation people in Wisconsin and Minnesota. In the large West Coast cities, as well as in cities closer to reservations elsewhere in the West, movement in and out of urban life is more fluid. It is clear, however, that in all major urban localities there are growing cores of permanently settled Indian families that continue to help Indians from the reservations gain more or less permanent places in city life.

The growing segment of settled city dwellers often regard themselves as members of the various reservation tribes, and in fact they are, by the established criteria. They not only maintain family ties and seek advice from elders on the reservations in regard to the technicalities of the traditional dances and music, but they also vote in the reservation communities and promote their political interests in tribal affairs. When tribes have won their claims before the Indian Claims Commission, the urban people have often clashed with reservation residents. Usually they have opposed using the funds for reservation development, as urged by the BIA and many tribal majorities on reservations; instead, they vote for per capita payments. On other issues there are also differences between urban and reservation people, and sometimes there have been protracted struggles for political power between factions on and off reservations, as among the Potawatomis. In this respect, as in the matter of militancy and civil rights, a new element has been injected into reservation life as a result of the steady growth of the urban segment.

These differences extend also to the relationship with the federal government. In 1972 an organization called the National American Indian Council was founded by Indians representing Indian centers in San Francisco. The council took a strong position in urging the government to assume responsibilities for off-reservation Indians comparable to those it maintains for reservation residents. There were also court cases supporting extension of specific services. Thus, the federal government—Indian relationship was in process of change during the 1970s, a direct result of the rapid urban shift in the Indian population.

FEDERAL POLICY TOWARD AMERICAN INDIANS

The policy of the U.S. government toward American Indians can be separated into five distinct periods, reflecting shifting views of Indians specifically and of the place of ethnic groups generally in American life. These periods may be summarized as follows: (1) separation, during which the prime objective was to remove Indians from the land that whites desired and draw boundaries between the two peoples; (2) coercive assimilation, during which whites sought to replace Indian ways with their own ways and to help them become self-sufficient farmers and artisans, under conditions dictated by whites; (3) tribal restoration, phase I, during which whites made an about-face and encouraged Indians to maintain their corporate tribal existence if they chose to do so; (4) termination, during which the objective was to break off all relationships of protection and assistance with the federal government; and (5) tribal restoration, phase II, during which tribal corporate adaptation to American society was again encouraged and cultural choice was reaffirmed. The long second period of cultural assimilation and the short fourth period of termination are related and must be understood as expressions of a persistent tendency in American society.

During the first century of U.S. independence, the idea prevailed that Indians were a separate, not an integral, part of the political society. Apparently not considered in the Declaration of Independence among "all men . . . created equal," Indians were only once mentioned in the Constitution (in connection with the regulation of commerce with foreign countries), and Indians were not admitted to citizenship, except a few by special treaty provision, until after 1887. The principle of separation was enunciated by President James Monroe in 1825 and embodied in the Indian Removal Act of 1830.

By the 1880s a different view was evolving, that Indians should be incorporated rapidly into American society whether they wished it or not. The Dawes Act of 1887 and the Curtis Act of 1898 defined the means for achieving this and were supplemented by directives of the Bureau of Indian Affairs (BIA), beginning as early as 1873, aimed at the complete replacement of Indian cultures. This policy prevailed into the 1920s, and in 1924 Congress granted citizenship to all Indians.

However, a view emerged during the 1920s that Indians should not be coerced into discarding their cultural traditions, a position embodied in the Indian Reorganization Act (IRA), passed in 1934, which recognized the right of Indians to their own local government on the reservations. Also, the BIA encouraged freedom of choice in religion and other aspects of life. This new approach was based on the concept that distinctive Indian ways could be expected to exist indefinitely, reversing the view that Indian cultures were dying out.

In the 1950s a reaction set in against the policy inaugurated by the IRA. Actions of Congress, beginning with a House Resolution in 1953, defined a new approach, which sought to eliminate reservations and end the special relationship between Indians and the federal government through the BIA. The policy, labeled termination, was vigorously opposed by almost all Indians. It also aroused strong negative reactions both within and outside of Congress.

In 1961 the new administration repudiated the termination program, as did each successive administration into the 1970s. In 1973 Congress restored the working relationship between the BIA and the Menominee Tribe, one of the few that had been terminated. The trend through the 1970s was to affirm and develop further the provisions of the IRA. A major landmark in the reinstituted policy came in 1975 with the passage of what became known as the Indian Self-Determination Act.

The general trend of Indian policy has been toward increasing acceptance of Indians as part of the body politic, but during the 20th century there have been sharply differing views as to how their role should be defined. These striking shifts of policy cannot be understood apart from general trends in the United States and the Western world. The political exclusion of Indians, their subjection to a powerfully implemented cultural assimilation program, the restoration of local government and freedom of cultural choice, the effort to place integration on an individual rather than a group basis in the termination program, with subsequent reaffirmation of ethnic group existence—each of these policies respecting integration into the nation-state has parallels in attitudes toward black, European immigrant, and other ethnic groups in the United States. From a still broader viewpoint, U.S. Indian policy has unquestionably been influenced by ethnic group policies in Great Britain, Spain, France, and other Western nations, especially during the 19th and 20th centuries.

Separation

The roots of the earliest U.S. policy lay in the British colonial experience and grew out of the struggle for land that immediately developed between Indians and the English. Some of the early invaders bought land, thus recognizing the Indians as rightful possessors, while others merely squatted where they landed and continued to expand their holdings, ignoring prior Indian possession. Once the Europeans gained a foothold, a fairly consistent official policy emerged in various agreements between Indians and colonists in Virginia, Pennsylvania, New England, and elsewhere. It was most clearly embodied in the Proclamation of 1763, at the close of the French and Indian War. Two principles were implicit: the Indian peoples, or nations, as they were usually called, were political entities to be dealt with as the British customarily dealt with territory-controlling nations in Europe, that is, by diplomacy, warfare, and treaty; and conflict would be prevented if there were clear boundaries between colonists and Indians that the central government would control. The proclamation set a boundary along the crest of the Appalachians, west of which Indians could enjoy their lands in peace. The statement also affirmed by implication the legality of British possession of the lands east of the line as a *fait accompli*.

The cornerstone of British policy was thus the idea of defined and respected boundaries, adjusted when necessary by treaties. It established an honorable tradition of discussion and mutual agreement. After the United States won its independence, Secretary of War Henry Knox was given the responsibility for developing Indian policy. He conscientiously sought to establish a policy of "liberal justice" in dealing with Indians, basing his efforts on the British separation principle. In the Indian trade and intercourse acts that Congress passed between 1790 and 1796 as their first significant policy statements, the concept of "Indian country" was established, and congressional regulation of Indian–white relations affirmed. The paradoxical concept of a people within the territory of the new nation and yet outside the processes of its political life was beginning to take form.

This troublesome principle was expressed by the Supreme Court in 1831. During the previous decade friction and what amounted to border warfare had developed between the Cherokees and the other residents of Georgia. The Indians' territory was demarcated by treaties, but the Georgians refused to recognize Indian jurisdiction over the land and claimed the right to enter the territory and administer their own laws. Invasions of the Cherokee territory became increasingly frequent when gold was discovered there in 1828. The Cherokee Nation brought suit against the state, asking for an injunction to restrain Georgians from attempting to apply the laws of the state within Cherokee territory. The case reached the U.S. Supreme Court, which ruled that the Cherokee Nation had "an unquestioned right to the lands they occupy" but denied the injunction on the ground that the court could not "control the legislature of Georgia." However, this equivocal decision included Chief Justice John Marshall's definition of the tribes as "dependent domestic nations" within the United States, a definition that became a source of ideas about the legal status of the Indians.

In an 1833 decision, in a case of a missionary living within the Cherokee Nation who was abducted by officers of Georgia and sentenced to hard labor under the laws of that state, Marshall made his concept of "dependent domestic nation" much clearer. He wrote in the court's decision: "The very term 'nation,' so generally applied to them [the Indians], means 'a people distinct from other.' The constitution by declaring treaties already made, as well as those to be made, to be the supreme law of the land, had adopted and sanctioned the previous treaties with the Indian nations, and, consequently, admits their rank among those Powers who are capable of making treaties." Marshall also specifically affirmed certain rights of Indians within their bounded territories: "These articles [asserted in treaties] are associated with others, recognizing their title to self government. The very fact of repeated treaties with them recognized it; and the settled doctrine of the law of nations is, that a weaker power does not surrender its independence—its right to self government—by associating with a stronger, and taking its protection." The decision nullified Georgia's action against the missionary and in so doing affirmed principles of policy that have not been superseded by later decisions.

Thus, by the 1830s American policy toward the Indians had been defined in some detail. Its ultimate legislative expression may be taken to be the Indian Removal Act of 1830, which in the tradition of the Proclamation of 1763 proposed to remove Indians to the sparsely populated country west of the Mississippi River for their own protection and the welfare of the United States. However, this was not to be done without the Indians' consent. There were to be negotiations and land exchanges. Appropriate payments were to be made, and the Indians were to be free to continue or set up local governments as they saw fit in the new lands assigned to them. Every removal was to be based on a mutual agreement, the conditions of which were to be duly recorded in a treaty signed by both the Indians and the federal government. In fact, though, tribes reluctant to move west were subjected to heavy pressures to do so. By the 1850s the removal policy had been applied in such a way as to move the Indian–white frontier west beyond the tier of new states on the west bank of the Mississippi. The old frontier problems had not been eliminated but merely moved to new locations.

Separation continued to be the guiding principle for another quarter of a century, although it was becoming clear that the sweeping approach of the Proclamation of 1763 as embodied in the Indian Removal Act would have to be abandoned. The vision of a distant Indian country, sufficiently remote so that border clashes could be avoided by drawing boundaries, was no longer realistic. There were Indians and white settlers everywhere in the West. True enough, there was Indian Territory, established in 1825, resulting from removal of the Five Civilized Tribes (as whites referred to the Cherokees, Choctaws, Creeks, Chickasaws, and Seminoles) and many other Indian groups. But it was recognized that the concentration in Indian Territory could not increase much more, and white settlers were pushing in there as well.

The principle of separation was now applied piecemeal in the form of the reservation system, which spelled out specific boundaries for each newly conquered tribe. A separate treaty with each of the scores of tribes brought under U.S. control was necessary to designate their new reservation, usually a portion of the territory they had roamed or had settled on. Although the idea of reservations was not new, having been used from colonial times, what was new was the realization that the hope of an "Indian country" truly separate geographically from white society had become impossible to sustain. White society had to reckon with Indian tribes within its midst, and dependent domestic nations scattered widely throughout the United States began to seem anomalous. Moreover, the Indians were now powerless, as the U.S. Cavalry supervised the settling of once-formidable tribes into the reservations. The result of the new conditions was a radical change in policy. By 1887 the tradition of negotiation with Indian tribes was dead, and unilateral government action had come to be regarded as perfectly appropriate. Even at the time Chief Justice Marshall was formulating a policy of negotiation, an opposite, unilateral approach was developing.

President Andrew Jackson undertook the administration of the Removal Act after 1830. He had earlier declared that he believed treaty-making with Indians to be absurd. A frontiersman and experienced Indian fighter who held that only military power worked, he proceeded to follow the letter but not the spirit of the law in furthering Indian removal. Anxious to remove the Cherokees and the other Civilized Tribes of the southern states, he sought out any handful of Indians who would sign a removal treaty without considering whether the signers represented the tribe as a whole. In this respect, Jackson was a precursor of the new era in Indian affairs. The viewpoint was reinforced in 1871, when Congress voted to abandon the policy of making any treaties with Indians. In 1872 Secretary of the Interior Columbus Delano formulated the view that had by then become dominant: "In our intercourse with the Indians it must always be borne in mind that we are the most powerful party . . . we assume that it is our duty to coerce them, if necessary, into the adoption and practice of our habits and customs." From a policy of recognition of Indians as near equals, with whom negotiation respecting their affairs was important and necessary, the U.S. government moved to a position from which Indians were seen as subordinate and indeed no more to be consulted with than children.

Coercive Assimilation

Faced with tens of thousands of Indians on large areas of highly coveted land, who were rendered dependent both legally and physically, as their former means of subsistence were much reduced or wholly destroyed, Congress began during the 1880s to formulate new policy objectives within the framework of "coercion if necessary." To this end Congress was strongly influenced, not by consultations with Indians as to their needs, but rather by the views of various well-meaning religious groups. Most of the Christian denominations had had some experience with Indians. In colonial times missionaries had spent years in efforts to convert them, to reduce their languages to writing, and to provide schools. Many religious groups had received specific government sanction to work on particular reservations during President Ulysses S. Grant's peace policy of the 1860s, which was designed to encourage persuasion rather than military force in the effort to get Indians to settle on reservations. During the 1880s many religious persons with concern for Indians met annually at Lake Mohonk in New York State. Ideas from these and similar conferences crystallized into a coherent set of policy objectives, which were translated into the General Allotment, or Dawes, Act of 1887. This legislation, together with subsequent acts of Congress and regulations of the BIA, initiated the second phase of U.S. Indian policy.

In contrast with the separation policy that had prevailed until then, the predominant idea became assimilation or, as it was often phrased, the civilizing of the Indians. The General Allotment Act, drawn up specifically to make the Indians into white men, culturally speaking, assigned title to 160 acres to each family head. It was believed that individual responsibility for the land and for a family's welfare on it would promptly result in each Indian becoming a hardworking, economically motivated person like the thousands of white settlers who had spread across the land. At the same time, other Americans would profit; after all the Indian family heads had been assigned land, the United States could distribute the surplus to non-Indians, who were ready to take it up. The plan would solve at one stroke the problem of how to bring about the maximum utilization of the land, which had been a concern ever since the time of Jefferson.

Thus, one major policy objective was seen as the assimilation of Indians to white economic ways through redistribution of the land. A secondary, related goal was the elimination of Indian community and political organization. Most whites assumed that Indians were incapable of governing themselves or that they maintained corrupt and highly inefficient local governments, as had been developed, they believed, by the Five Civilized Tribes in Indian Territory. Whites understood that all Indian organization rested on collective, tribal holding of the land, which was regarded as a serious obstacle to their becoming civilized. Breaking up the land into individual parcels would bring about not only individual responsibility in economic affairs but also the elimination of the land base for tribal organization.

Land allotment was carried out by agents of the BIA, who treated Indian political organization as nonexistent, except in the cases of the Five Civilized Tribes, a few others of Indian Territory, and the Senecas of New York. The governments of these tribes were expected to negotiate with government officials to carry out allotment. When it became apparent that the Cherokees and Choctaws would not allow allotment and in fact brought suit in federal courts, Congress passed the Curtis Act of 1898, which dissolved those tribal governments as legal institutions. That legislation made it clear that the federal government was determined to act unilaterally and that no Indian governing bodies would be allowed to continue unless they obeyed the federal administrators.

The third objective of this second phase, although not embodied in either the Dawes or the Curtis acts, was based on stipulations in the Dawes Act that all Indians who received titles to their allotted land were to be granted U.S. citizenship, conditional on having "adopted the habits of civilized life." These habits apparently were assumed to be obvious, as they were not further defined in the act or in other federal legislation, and they probably were obvious to the white employees of the BIA; civilized habits were their own ways of behaving, that is, speaking English, wearing hair and clothing in the fashion of the period, working six days a week, going to a Christian church on Sunday, and so on. Coercing Indian children if necessary into these ways was the ultimate objective of the assimilation program.

From 1887 to 1934 the efforts of the BIA, supplemented by those of Christian churches, which were active on most reservations, were directed energetically to assimilation. Although the three objectives—replacing collective by individual landholding, eliminating Indian self-governing institutions, and replacing Indian cultural ways—were never fully realized, the effects on Indian lives were very great. This policy phase engendered the deepest distrust of the federal government and the maximum hostility toward whites.

During the first 25 to 30 years of the allotment program, Indians lost at least two-thirds of all their landholdings, not only through the sale to the United States of the surplus on each reservation after allotment, as provided for by law, but also through purchase and fraudulent deals by whites, who devised a great variety of means for acquiring the allotted land. In this way Indian ownership was reduced in many areas to small fractions of the land they had once held. In addition, many reservations were checkerboarded, that is, they became areas in which whites and Indians lived side by side, a circumstance that effectively interfered with Indian community life but rarely resulted in cooperative relations among Indians and whites. Eventually, after some 30 years of administrative complexities, the whole allotment program was abandoned, and large reservations in many parts of the West were never, or only to a limited extent, allotted. The northern plains and the Southwest, particularly, escaped allotment. By the 1920s it was clear that tens of thousands of Indians had not become farmers or ranchers according to the white model and that collective tribal ownership of land (with titles held in trust by the government in order to control the sale and prevent the loss of land) remained an important framework for the majority of Indians in the United States.

The Bureau of Indian Affairs, by creating an institution of its own—the superintendency—was much more successful in destroying local Indian institutions than in allotting all the land. Although agents of the government had been assigned to various administrative tasks among Indians ever since colonial times, during the coercive phase of Indian policy the field agents, called superintendents, sought to undermine their local governments and inhibit any autonomous community organization. The superintendent of a reservation or area of a former reservation, as in Oklahoma (formerly Indian Territory), ordinarily became the most powerful influence on local Indian affairs, even though he was a government employee, not responsible to the Indians but to his superiors in Washington. Through him came the assistance that the Indians needed for any kind of development, and through him usually were channeled all important relations with outsiders. Indians who cooperated with him received favors.

Thus, the administration of reservation affairs was carried out by a government employee surrounded by his Indian allies. In all but a few cases the superintendents despised the Indian local governments, as in the case of a superintendent among the Pueblos, who characterized their ancient institutions as "opera bouffé." Under these conditions, some once-flourishing tribal governments, like those of the Five Civilized Tribes, disappeared, and some, like the complex Pueblo institutions, operated in almost an underground status, or at least without an effective relationship with the federal government. In 1910 a commissioner of Indian affairs, voicing the viewpoint of the government policymakers of the time, wrote: "The Indian problem has now reached a stage where its solution is almost wholly a matter of administration." In other words, benevolent agents would now manage the affairs of Indians in accord with government regulations. Under the assimilation policy, Indian tribal government had been replaced, not with American representative democracy, but with administrative bureaucracy.

To an observer it might have appeared that the third objective of policy—the replacement of Indian ways by "the habits of civilized life"—had been largely successful from the 1880s to the early 1930s. During this half-century the changes in Indian lifestyles were certainly considerable. The majority of Indians in every part of the nation learned to speak English and adopted clothing and houses basically similar to those of neighboring whites; only a few tribes, such as the Pueblos and Navajos of the Southwest, maintained some traditional features of dress and housing. The most distinctive ways of making a living, such as buffalo hunting, raiding Mexican ranches, wild food gathering, or small-scale floodwater farming, were no longer possible and were replaced by wage work and other occupations of the industrial age. A closer look at Indian ways of life, however, reveals that fewer than a dozen of the Indian languages died out, many forms of Indian religious life and ceremonialism were vigorous, and Indians everywhere asserted that they lived by values distinct from and preferable to those of the majority of Americans.

These mixed results may be better understood in the light of the methods used to replace Indian cultures. Federally administered schools, supplemented to some extent by schools managed by the various religious denominations, were considered the chief tool for achieving assimilation. Even before the 1880s the boarding schools began to be regarded as playing a key role, because they separated children from the influence of their parents and of the Indian communities. According to BIA regulations, an important duty of superintendents was to keep the boarding schools full by any feasible means, such as withholding rations from parents if they refused to send their children voluntarily. Parents did resist, and there was coercion. The boarding schools were kept more or less full for nearly 50 years, and the children were often placed in white households during the summer in a determined effort to keep children in contact with white culture and out of contact with Indian culture. The techniques employed were indicated in 1908 by Richard H. Pratt, who founded Carlisle Indian School in Pennsylvania and who was called by whites the "Red Man's Moses": "The multiplicity of tribes represented enabled a mixing of tribes in dormitory rooms. The rooms held three to four each and it was arranged that no two of the same tribe were placed in the same room. This not only helped in the acquirement of English but broke up tribal and race clannishness, a most important victory in getting the Indian toward real citizenship." Such techniques were effective in diffusing knowledge of English and white ways among Indians as well as in broadening the horizons of Indian children beyond their own tribal boundaries. Many intertribal marriages resulted, and boarding-school Indians sometimes settled in white communities for many years. However, the major complaint of the federal educators during the early 20th century and before was that Indians everywhere were "going back to the blanket." By this they meant that despite the considerable experience of "civilized ways," Indians were choosing to live in Indian communities, that is, on reservations.

In general, it may be said that formal education away from home resulted more frequently in new problems of cultural conflict on reservations than in a steady flow of Indians out of the reservations into white society. The return to reservations with widened outlook often resulted in individual personality problems and in factional strife within Indian communities, as well as in acceptance of many features of white civilization. In addition, new hostilities developed toward whites and white ways, and it may be said that the policy of off-reservation education had many unanticipated consequences that the proponents themselves rated as undesirable.

Another element in the program for "civilizing" Indians consisted of encouraging Christian missionaries and suppressing the native religions. The missionaries were strikingly successful everywhere in gaining adherents to their many different churches, so that by the 1930s the great majority of Indians professed Christian church affiliation. However, certain of the native religions were still vigorous in the 1930s, such as those of the Pueblo Indians of New Mexico and the Navajos. In addition, new religions sprang up, especially during the period of most intensive suppression. The Native American church, which employs some Christian concepts and symbols along with the use of peyote, became well established from Oklahoma through the plains and ultimately in the Southwest. The Redbird Smith movement revitalized traditional Cherokee beliefs and became an important influence in eastern Oklahoma. The Indian Shaker church integrated traditional and Christian beliefs among thousands of Indians of different tribes in the Northwest. The Longhouse religion of the Iroquois continued its vigorous growth from its beginnings in 1800. In every region, Indians developed new religions, increasing the number of sects of the reservations.

In the mid-1920s the primarily destructive effects of the coercive assimilation policy attracted the attention of new policymakers in government and of private organizations concerned with Indian rights. The result was an extensive study of the condition of Indians on all reservations, undertaken not by the BIA or any other branch of government but by the Brookings Institution, an impartial private organization devoted to research into government operations and policies. Published in 1928, the study, entitled *The Problem of Indian Administration*, reported that on all fronts the assimilation program had failed to realize its objectives and that

Indians lived in conditions of extreme poverty, with poor health and inadequate education. The report recommended that the BIA recast entirely its approach to education and adapt its inadequate school system to the needs of Indians as members of U.S. society. The report, along with other, more specialized analyses, influenced the government to develop a radically different approach to Indian affairs.

The Indian Reorganization Act

During the early 1930s congressional committees worked on drafting new legislation to replace the policy of the 1880s. In 1934, under the innovative administration of Franklin D. Roosevelt, Congress passed the Indian Reorganization Act (IRA), defining a new framework for Indian policy. It aimed at reversing the effects of the General Allotment Act, the Curtis Act, and the succession of BIA regulations designed to force cultural assimilation. In some respects the new act reaffirmed the viewpoint of the Supreme Court in its decisions of the early 1830s.

The cultural distinctness of Indian communities was recognized as a fact, and no effort to alter that distinctness was made. The act provided for the restoration of some Indian lands and proposed means for recovery of some more, thus repudiating allotment, the basis of Indian policy since 1887. The IRA not only affirmed the importance of the reservations as a continuing land base but also reasserted the rights of Indians to govern themselves locally. Reversing the policy trend since 1871 of eliminating Indian political organization, the IRA made specific provision for tribal adoption of constitutions and election of representative councils.

This change represented a return to the Marshall doctrine that Indians had an inherent right to govern themselves within their own territory—but with a significant difference. The Marshall viewpoint was simply that Indians had the right to maintain their own governing institutions, which already existed at that time. The new legislation specifically proposed that the tribes adopt new institutions modeled on those of constitutional representative democracies. This was an advocacy of cultural assimilation with respect to political organization, but it was not coercive, in that Indians were not required to adopt the proposed form of government. The new policy also authorized Indian communities to organize as corporations for the management of tribal business enterprises. The new policy strove to relate reservation societies dynamically to the economic life of the nation.

These features of the IRA constituted a rejection of the Indian policy that had guided the U.S. government for more than half a century. They encouraged Indian communities to engage in landholding, politics, and economic development. The legislation resulted in immediate enlargement of some reservations and gave legal sanction to tribal landholding, officially recognizing the Indian land system as an existing institution rather than a disappearing phenomenon. These provisions of the IRA were far-reaching in their implications regarding the place of Indians as an ethnic group in American society. John Collier, the commissioner of Indian affairs who was appointed in 1932, wrote in a memorandum: "I see the broad function of Indian policy . . . to be the development of Indian democracy . . . The most significant clue to achieving full Indian democracy . . . is the continued survival, through all historical change and disaster, of the Indian tribal group, both as a reality and a legal entity." Such a view was at the opposite pole of opinion from that of nearly every Indian commissioner since the 1870s. Collier, who had been active in organizations working to define and protect Indian rights and to improve economic and other conditions on the reservations, regarded the new tribal councils, which nearly every tribe voted to organize during the 1930s and early 1940s, as training grounds for Indians to assume leadership and management of their own communities.

His administration also sought to define new goals for the federally administered school system. Day schools on the reservations were emphasized over boarding schools, although the latter continued to be the most important in the governmental education program. In both kinds of schools an effort was made to change the content of teaching so that Indian cultures were dealt with positively rather than ignored or disparaged. The new administration even introduced the teaching of Indian languages and prepared primers in three major tongues—the Navajo, a Pueblo, and a Siouan language. But these programs for a new orientation in the schools were not popular in Congress and in some respects turned out to be impracticable. Because of the inertia of the BIA and the hostility in Congress to spending government funds for teaching any language other than English and any history other than that of white Americans, there was little change in the schools by 1945, when Collier resigned in frustration.

Under the influence of the IRA, the effects of the hundred years of forced assimilation were not erased, of course, but important changes did begin. The superintendency as the arm of the BIA in reservation life continued, as did many constructive programs begun in the previous policy phase, such as the building of irrigation systems, the development of Indian-owned cattle herds, the expansion of crafts production, and the exploitation of oil, natural gas, and other minerals on reservations. However, Indians began to participate in planning and management through tribal councils and council committees. The BIA retained control because of its annual appropriations from Congress and its trained personnel, but many tribal councils began to act with some degree of independent leadership and forced the BIA to take them into account. Some superintendents believed in the new policy and tried to bring Indians increasingly into management and policymaking at the reservation level. The effects of the IRA were mixed with respect to the degree of Indian participation in shaping their destiny, but there was no doubt that immediately after 1934 new political processes were stimulated, which had not been true during the long period of coercive policy. There was a tendency toward growth of the representative democracy that Commissioner Collier envisioned.

In addition, political action by Indians outside the purely local sphere revived intertribal organizations in a way that had not been apparent since before the General Allotment Act had gone into operation in Indian Territory. With the Collier administration's encouragement, Indian leaders in 1944 founded the National Congress of American Indians (NCAI), an intertribal association whose varied program included lobbying in Congress and correcting misleading stereotypes of Indians. The NCAI, beginning with leadership by Cherokees and other groups from eastern Oklahoma, steadily increased in size and influence to become an important political force among all tribes of the United States.

Consistent with these developments, Congress in 1946 established an Indian Claims Commission. This was a product of the deep and widespread sentiment among Americans generally that Indians had been dealt with unjustly throughout American history, especially with respect to their land. The commission was empowered to hear cases brought by a tribe and to provide compensation for proven illegal or unjust losses. During the next 30 years the commission judged many cases and awarded millions of dollars. The common effort to prepare claims cases brought new solidarity in many tribes but also new factionalism, arising in some cases from the distribution of compensation funds. Cases before the commission were still being settled in the 1970s.

In the first phase of this new policy, during which tribal restoration was the dominant principle, organized corporations developed widely among Indian tribes. New forms of organization within and among tribes grew and became instruments for economic and political initiatives. The Indians' economic and health conditions continued at very low levels as compared with the general U.S. population, but the level of formal education rose somewhat, and the Indian population, which had reached an all-time low in the late 19th century, was on the increase in nearly all groups.

Termination

Support for the earlier policy of coercive assimilation did not disappear with the passage of the IRA, however. In most sessions of Congress bills to abolish the reservations were proposed. A good many Americans thought that reservations were a species of concentration camp, and that the Indians should be set free. Conflicts of jurisdiction between tribal councils and county governments and between the BIA and the states embodied the contradictions built into Indian policy. During the early 1950s these viewpoints began to dominate in Congress, and policy was formulated that opposed the IRA and its associated programs. During President Dwight Eisenhower's administration there was an attempt to get the federal government "out of the Indian business." In 1953 the House and Senate approved a resolution calling for an end to the Indians' "status as wards of the United States" and specifying that certain tribes "should be freed from Federal supervision." Among these were two large tribes whose reservations contained important stands of timber—the Menominees in Wisconsin and the Klamaths in Oregon. Paying lip service to Indian consent, as in the 1830s, the federal government proceeded to sever its connection with the designated tribes under a policy that came to be called termination.

The Indians, when pushed to vote on termination, were split into factions. The majority did not understand the issues, as became apparent later. When they realized what the results of termination would be, namely, loss of control of their timber lands, some groups sought to reverse the action. The Menominees in 1973 were ultimately successful in reestablishing their federal relationship, whereas the Klamaths remained terminated. The policy of termination, which was rejected when the administration in Washington changed after the 1960 election, aroused strong, widespread negative reaction in the United States among non-Indians as well as almost universal, active opposition by Indians.

Tribal Restoration

After that, policy again moved in the new-old directions pointed by the IRA. The most notable addition—community action programs—emerged during President Lyndon Johnson's administration in the 1960s. The community action programs on the reservations, administered by the Indian Desk of the Office of Economic Opportunity (OEO), introduced new organizations that supplemented the tribal councils, which in many cases had become merely administrative arms of the superintendencies. The new programs introduced three features: the training of Indian citizens in action programs; the creation of responsible committees for making decisions about the use of federal funds; and in some instances, contracts between Indian communities and the OEO for the administration of development programs. These provisions were in the spirit of the IRA goal of reestablishing effective community organization among Indians, for they tended to transfer decision making from the BIA to the Indian communities. The new arrangements often challenged those tribal councils that had been overwhelmed by the superintendency and had not worked for maximum independence. The making of contracts specifically opened the way to a new approach by encouraging participation of Indians in the management of their reservations, which the BIA had not been capable of doing.

The OEO and its community action committees were liquidated during the early 1970s, but the spirit in which they had been formulated continued. In 1970 the administration of President Richard Nixon announced its Indian policy: "Self-determination among the Indian people can and must be encouraged without the threat of eventual termination . . . This is the only way that self-determination can effectively be fostered . . . This, then, must be the goal of any new national policy toward the Indian people: to strengthen the Indians' sense of autonomy without threatening the sense of community . . . we must assure the Indian that he can assume control of his own life without being separated involuntarily from the tribal group. And we must make it clear that Indians can become independent of Federal control without being cut off from Federal concern and Federal support." In the spirit of this presidential message, Congress in 1975 passed the Indian Self-determination Act. It appeared that the change in Indian policy marked by the IRA in 1934 had inaugurated a long-term trend and that the termination legislation of the 1950s was but a brief interlude.

By the 1970s two opposing views existed, one that saw Indians as "just like everybody else" and therefore to be "melted" into American society as individuals, and another that saw Indian group distinctiveness within the whole of the United States as of high value and therefore to be nurtured. The general public was ambivalent and confused, and opinion tended to swing successively in different directions. Indian policy was a dynamic political issue that certainly was not stabilized by the 1970s.

Indian Initiatives

During the various changes in government policy, Indians did not stand by passively; they also developed policy of their own. In the early separation period under the British, the major reaction of the Indians was to build confederations of tribes. The Iroquois and, on a smaller scale, the Abnakis, the Wampanoags, and some others formed political confederacies in the Northeast and resisted white pressures to acquire their land. The Creeks and the Pamunkeys in the Southeast acted similarly, but none of these, not even the powerful Iroquois League, was able to stand against the military power of the whites. By the time of American independence, all the confederations had broken down.

Nevertheless, as the Americans vigorously pursued separation and removal, the policy of Indian unity reached an even broader expression than during British dominance. The Shawnee leader Tecumseh (1768–1813) by 1811 conceived of unity among all the tribes of the North and South. He preached personally to all the many displaced groups of the Northwest Territory to cease selling their land, to hold on to it, and to resist all pressures. Tecumseh urged his policy goals on his own Algonkian-speaking peoples, and he traveled south to influence the once-powerful Creeks and the rising Cherokees. He was eloquent, and his policy was clearly formulated and strongly presented, but he was not successful; only one small faction of the Creeks joined the Northwestern tribes. In the war between Tecumseh's supporters and the federal government that began with the battle of Tippecanoe, the Indians were crushed and Tecumseh was killed.

Military resistance by confederacies was not the only policy that guided Indians faced with the determined separation and removal policy. As President Andrew Jackson moved under the authority of the Removal Act to push the Civilized Tribes of the Southeast out of the white man's way, some of the Cherokee leaders decided to resist by lobbying in Washington, by appealing for justice to the general American public, and by appealing to the federal courts. This policy, vigorously pursued by John Ross (1790–1866) and other Cherokee leaders, also failed. All of the Five Civilized Tribes were forced by U.S. troops to abandon their peaceful program of resistance.

By the time the forced assimilation policy had crystallized in the 1880s, Indians everywhere had capitulated to white military power and were in various stages of adaptation to life on the reservations. Their struggle for control of the land had been lost, and white power was being employed to divest them of still more land. Indian hopes reached a low, and Indian political leadership lost momentum; only the Cherokees, Creeks, and Choctaws maintained some vision and strength.

For the most part, Indian leadership now appeared in religious life; it was the religious prophets who set their goals. Among the Indians removed from the Great Lakes area, among the newly demobilized Plains Indians, among the Northwest Coast people, prophets arose, telling of promised lands where the old ways could be renewed without white domination. Wovoka (c. 1856–1932), the Messiah of the Paiutes in Nevada, spread the Ghost Dance across the West; the power of that religion frightened the whites into the massacre at Wounded Knee, S.Dak., which became a burning symbol for both Indians and whites. The peyote cult and, in the Northwest, Smohalla's vision were typical responses in this period of declining hopes in the material world. Policy was ritualized and dealt with the spiritual world instead. Many of these visionary religions became permanent and continued to give guidance, as in the Native American church. However, even the religious spirit was overwhelmed in the assimilation phase. White control was so well established that not only was military resistance impossible, but the spiritual world itself seemed conquered.

It was under these conditions that whites offered the new policy of tribal restoration. The Indians' acquiescence to the tribal council system may be regarded as the beginning of a new policy era for them, in which they generally accepted their assigned role within the American social system. No longer socially and politically separate, no longer able to take refuge in visionary worlds, the Indians set goals within the white-dominated society and utilized the institutions of that society to realize them. The limits of policy were somewhat expanded, both within and outside of the reservations. This kind of widespread involvement in the dominant institutions had been foreshadowed more than a hundred years earlier by the Cherokees just prior to removal to Indian Territory, when they built political institutions modeled on those of the whites.

The termination phase was too short for much Indian-formulated policy to develop, although they generally opposed it. Despite long-standing resentment of BIA methods, they viewed the bureau as their only bulwark against what they believed to be the continuing desire of their immediate neighbors to acquire Indian land and wipe out their cultural differences. Moreover, the feeling was strong among Indians generally that the U.S. government owed them a great deal for taking nearly all their land and for failing to live up to the many treaties as settlers moved across the continent. Thus, termination was strongly opposed on the ground that the federal government had not equipped the Indians to resist successfully the ever-present pressures for eliminating them as a people. If termination policy had continued longer, many different tribes undoubtedly would have organized the kind of action that resulted in Congress rescinding the Menominee termination program.

When the tribal restoration policy resumed after 1960, the Indians pursued some distinctive new policies. For tens of thousands on reservations, there was no essential change, but since World War II there were also tens of thousands of Indians who no longer lived permanently on reservations, who had migrated to cities in every part of the country. A considerable number of off-reservation dwellers were or had been college students. These people, removed from the more conservative influences of the tribal council communities, developed new ideas about the place of Indians in American society. Political militancy grew during the 1960s, and younger Indian leaders in California, Minnesota, and elsewhere organized demonstrations to acquaint the American public with conditions on and off the reservations. An early action consisted of an attempt in 1969 to take over Alcatraz Island, the former federal prison in San Francisco Bay; claims that it was legitimate Indian land were advanced, and short-lived efforts were made to establish a training school for Indians on the island. The young and militant Indian leadership then organized more demonstrations, including a march on Washington in 1972, called the Trail of Broken Treaties, and the occupation of the BIA building in Washington the same year. In 1973 leaders of the American Indian Movement (AIM) took over the small community of Wounded Knee, where violence erupted between federal officials and Indians. The Indians' militancy paralleled that of blacks and Mexican Americans during the 1960s.

Other forms of action during the late 1960s and 1970s included a kind of cultural renaissance and new legal actions, both guided by new, specialized, nonpolitical associations. A group of Indians in San Francisco organized an Indian Historical Society for the purpose of writing and publishing history from the Indian, rather than the white, point of view. They published a journal called *The Indian Historian*, encouraged Indians to write for it, and printed articles about Indian history that contrasted greatly with those published in the usual scholarly journals. An Indian Press Association released to newspapers and magazines news about Indian affairs that often varied considerably from news of the same events disseminated by the wire services. These and other activities that flourished during the 1960s and 1970s were initiated with funds from various private foundations and individuals; they constituted an area of Indian life in which the federal government played no role at all, in sharp contrast to the reservations, where the government's role was still very prominent.

With private funds the Native American Rights Fund was founded in Colorado. Among other activities, it researched legal aspects of the many land cessions made by Indians since colonial times and discovered that a number of such cessions were apparently illegal. When East Coast states such as Maine and Massachusetts had pushed through cessions of land from the Passamaquoddy, Wampanoag-Mashpee, Narragansett, and other groups, they had bypassed Congress, the only body that had the legal power to carry out such negotiations. With legal guidance from the Native American Rights Fund, tribes brought suits against the states, and during the 1970s a number of such cases were being adjudicated. One in Massachusetts involved the very small group of Mashpee Indians, which a jury decided had not been constituted as a tribe at the time the state took over their land; the court suspended judgment, and the case was then appealed. It appeared that in the future the policy of the Indians would be to avoid jury trial. Instead, their strategy would be negotiation by lawyers with specialized knowledge. The fact that these cases were taken to court rather than to the Indian Claims Commission indicated a new role for Indians, much freer from control by the administrative arm of the government.

The fullest understanding of U.S. Indian policy comes through comparison with the policies of other modern nation-states for dealing with ethnic groups in their territories. To some degree, governments of the West went through similar developments in ethnic policy from the 1600s to the 1970s. A not-uncommon policy before the 19th century was separation of a conquering group and the conquered natives. This policy was practiced by the English after their conquest of the Irish, when a pale of settlement was established at the River Shannon in 1653, and all English-speaking persons who behaved like Englishmen and rejected Irish ways were enjoined to live east of the Shannon; those who spoke Gaelic and clung to Irish modes of dress and other customs were required to live west of the line. Earlier the Romans had set patterns in this regard in Britain and in the Iberian peninsula. The Romans and Romanized persons lived in the cities, while the barbarians lived beyond the cities' bounds. European countries during the Middle Ages had clearly bounded ghettos for Jews, and Russia had a well-established rural pale of settlement in the 19th century. Separation policy was not universal, but some form of it appeared in most European states as an accepted means for keeping apart the conquered natives or immigrants, regarded as below the cultural level of the dominant group that controlled the state apparatus.

Again we can turn to English policy in Ireland for a parallel with the U.S. policy. The pale of settlement kept "civilized" peoples and barbarians from mingling, but it did not necessarily keep English and Irish apart; many Irish men and women took on English ways, from language and dress to religion and world view. Nevertheless, a hundred years after the pale was set up, a majority of Irish continued to reject the English language, the Anglican church, and most other English ways. The English response was ultimately to take vigorous steps to assimilate the Irish culturally. Many legal devices were tried, but in the 19th century something like the U.S. government's Indian school policy was adopted —not boarding schools separating parents and children, but national schools in which the Gaelic language and Irish history were ignored; the schools were wholly English in language and outlook. Irish Catholicism came under fire, and an organized effort to Anglicize the religion was instituted. It was indeed a coercive assimilation policy, if not so drastic in method as that in the United States, and proceeded on the same assumption, namely, that English culture was superior in all respects to Irish culture and had to be adopted for the good of the Irish. In many European countries during the 19th century assimilation programs were instituted, often using less drastic means than the English or Americans, but with the same goals. Efforts to introduce a standard language and to teach a national history were essentially aimed at replacing the many languages and cultural identities of European peoples who did not belong to the dominant ethnic group controlling the government. Catalan, Basque, Flemish, various Germanic and Slavic languages were labeled as inferior and not officially recognized, although they were spoken by millions of people. The assimilation policies promulgated by the ethnic groups in power grew out of the idea that the nation-state should be culturally homogeneous and were part of Europe's colonial expansion phase, which rested strongly on the concept of racial and cultural superiority.

The tribal restoration policy in the United States was instituted in the aftermath of World War I and it may be regarded as related to the influence of discussions about the Versailles Peace Treaty, in which President Woodrow Wilson became the spokesman for the rights of minorities and for self-determination of European ethnic groups. The restoration of independence and the expansion of self-determination were in the air in the Western world. Ireland won independence; it was seen that Europe's colonies would inevitably become new nations. President Wilson maintained a blind spot with reference to the self-determination of American Indians, but the Indian policy of the 1930s formulated by others was in the spirit of his proposed changes in the map of Europe.

However, the United States was an integrationist rather than a pluralist state; that is to say, its political structure was wholly individualistic. In contrast with some other Western states, such as Switzerland, it had never given political recognition to any ethnic group as such within its borders (except for the Indians). The United States was ready by 1924 to grant full citizenship to Indians, but on an exclusively individual basis. Its basic law could not be construed as sanctioning any role for ethnic groups in its political structure. It was this political standpoint that was the foundation of the termination policy.

Nevertheless, Indians had been recognized as distinct ethnic groups holding land collectively, and in the 1934 legislation Congress formalized these groups as having a kind of political existence under the tribal councils. In its tribal restoration policy, the government was consistently moving with one strong trend of the times, an important tendency of post-World War I Europe and the former colonial world. Following the brief interlude of termination in 1954, the U.S. Congress continued vigorously the tribal restoration policy, a major action being the Indian Self-Determination Act of 1975.

BIBLIOGRAPHY

The standard reference for all tribes and their locations is J.R. Swanton, *The Indian Tribes of North America* (1952; reprint, Washington, D.C., 1969). Uniquely useful for recent populations both on and off reservations is Sol Tax, Samuel Stanley, and Robert K. Thomas, *The North American Indians, Distribution of the Descendants of the Aboriginal Population of Alaska, Canada, and the United States* (Chicago, 1961). For aboriginal populations, although it is currently questioned, A.L. Kroeber, *Cultural and Natural Areas of Native North America* (1939; reprint, Berkeley, 1963) is still the most useful. Of the several histories that attempt to cover the whole range of time and cultural variety, Ruth Underhill, *Red Man's America: A History of the Indians of the United States* (1953; reprint, Chicago, 1971), focuses on cultural traits, and E.H. Spicer, *A Short History of the Indians of the United States* (New York, 1969), focuses on Indian–white relations. Robert K. Thomas, "Pan-Indianism," in Stuart Levine and N.O. Lurie, eds., *The American Indian Today* (Deland, Fla., 1968), and *Red Power: The American Indian's Fight for Freedom* compiled by A.M. Josephy, Jr. (New York, 1970), sketch political movements and other cultural processes of the mid-20th century.

Peoples of the Atlantic Coast

The only introductory survey of history and cultural changes among the coastal Algonkians is T.J.C. Brasser, "The Coastal Algonkians: People of the First Frontiers," in Eleanor B. Leacock and Nancy O. Lurie, eds., *North American Indians in Historical Perspective* (New York, 1971). Two valuable cultural histories detailing processes of change and tribal persistence are T. Stern, *Chickahominy: The Changing Culture of a Virginia Indian Community* (Philadelphia, 1952), and E. Boissevain, "Narragansett Survival, A Study of Group Persistence through Adopted Traits," in Deward

E. Walker, ed., *The Emergent Native Americans* (Boston, 1972). For the early history of Indian–white contacts, see Alden T. Vaughan, *New England Frontier: Puritans and Indians, 1620–1675* (Boston, 1965), and Francis Jennings, *The Invasion of America* (Chapel Hill, N.C., 1975). For an Indian viewpoint on the history and culture of once-important Massachusetts Indian groups, see Milton A. Travers, *The Wampanoag Indian Federation: Indian Neighbors of the Pilgrims* (Boston, 1961).

The Depopulated Southeast

Most useful on the few surviving tribes in the Southeast are John Gulick, *Cherokees at the Crossroads* (Chapel Hill, N.C., 1960); W.C. Sturtevant, "Creek into Seminole," in E.B. Leacock and N.O. Lurie, eds., *North American Indians in Historical Perspective* (New York, 1971); and Charles M. Hudson, *The Catawba Nation* (Athens, Ga., 1970). Adolph L. Dial and David K. Eliades, *The Only Land I Know: A History of the Lumbee Indians* (San Francisco, 1975), gives an Indian view of the history of this controversial tribe.

The Iroquois of the Eastern Great Lakes Country

Edmund Wilson gives a penetrating description, together with relevant history, of 20th-century Iroquois life in *Apologies to the Iroquois* (New York, 1960). Anthony F. Wallace, *The Death and Rebirth of the Seneca* (New York, 1970), is a classic cultural history of one Iroquois tribe. More technical, but indispensable for basic understanding of Iroquois life, is A.A. Shimony, *Conservatism among the Iroquois at the Six Nations Reserve* (New Haven, Conn., 1961).

The Western Great Lakes Country

Of the many studies of Great Lakes peoples, past and present, the following constitute an introduction to four major types of cultural development. Harold Hickerson, *The Southwestern Chippewa: An Ethnohistorical Study* (1962; reprint, New York, 1971), sketches the complex history of the most numerous people of the region, while Victor Barnouw, *Acculturation and Personality among the Wisconsin Chippewa* (1950; reprint, New York, 1971), gives an introduction to the changing Chippewa culture. Felix Keesing, *The Menominee In-*

dians of Wisconsin, A Study of Three Centuries of Culture Contact and Change (1939; reprint, New York, 1971), is an analysis of long-term cultural processes. Nancy O. Lurie, ed., *Mountain Wolf Woman, Sister of Crashing Thunder: The Autobiography of a Winnebago Indian* (Ann Arbor, Mich., 1961), interprets a culture through one individual's experience of it. The Oneidas, a transplanted Iroquois group, are described in R.E. Ritzen- thaler, "The Oneida Indians of Wisconsin," *Bulletin of the Public Museum of the City of Milwaukee* 19 (1950): 1–52.

The Mississippi Valley

Many histories of the tribes removed or native to the lands west of the Mississippi are now available, especially in the Civilization of the American Indian Series published by the University of Oklahoma Press. One of these is A.M. Gibson, *The Kickapoos: Lords of the Middle Border* (Norman, Okla., 1963). Two studies of another transplanted people of the Mississippi River Valley are N.F. Joffe, "The Fox Indians of Iowa," in Ralph Linton, ed., *Acculturation in Seven American Indian Tribes* (1940; reprint, Gloucester, Mass., 1963), and F.O. Gearing, *The Face of the Fox* (Chicago, 1970). Margaret Mead, *The Changing Culture of An Indian Tribe* (1932; reprint, New York, 1971) describes the Omahas.

The Crucible of Oklahoma

A most useful introduction to the mélange of peoples now living in Oklahoma is Muriel H. Wright, *A Guide to the Indian Tribes of Oklahoma* (1951; reprint, Norman, Okla., 1965). Outstanding in its employment of documents and direct observations to unravel the complex history of a modern Oklahoma group is C.A. Weslager, *The Delaware Indians: A History* (New Brunswick, N.J., 1972). Angie Debo, *The Road to Disappearance: A History of the Creek Indians* (1941; reprint, Norman, Okla., 1967), is one of several fine histories by this author of the Five Civilized Tribes. Marion I. Starkey, *The Cherokee Nation* (1946; reprint, New York, 1972), is a highly readable account of this important and influential eastern Oklahoma tribe. Ernest Wallace and E.A. Hoebel, *The Comanches, Lords of the South Plains* (Norman, Okla., 1952), combine the techniques of historian and ethnologist in an account of the history and culture of a western Oklahoma tribe. Two very different accounts of the Pawnees are valuable: Gene Weltfish, *The Lost Universe* (New York, 1965), and "The Pawnee: Horsemen and Farmers of the Prairies," in Wendell Oswalt, *This Land Was Theirs: A Study of the North American Indian* (New York, 1973).

The Northern Plains

Gordon Macgregor, *Warriors without Weapons: A Study of the Society and Personality Development of the Pine Ridge Sioux* (Chicago, 1946), is a classic study of the most numerous and most famous people of the northern plains. Ethel Nurge, ed., *The Modern Sioux: Social Systems and Reservation Culture* (Lincoln, Nebr., 1970), expands the view of the Sioux to all the tribes and recounts more recent developments. Vine Deloria, Jr., *Custer Died for Your Sins: An Indian Manifesto* (New York, 1969), presents a modern Sioux's view of Indian affairs. John C. Ewers, *The Blackfeet: Raiders of the Northwestern Plains* (1958; reprint, Norman, Okla., 1967), relates the cultural history of another important northern plains group.

The Western Border of the Plains

Robert Emmitt, *The Last War Trail: The Utes and the Settlement of Colorado* (1954; reprint, Norman, Okla., 1972), is an effective portrayal of the impact of whites on Utes in the frontier period. Jack S. Harris, "The White Knife Shoshoni," in Ralph Linton, ed., *Acculturation in Seven American Indian Tribes* (1940; reprint, Gloucester, Mass., 1963), describes a group of the widely scattered Great Basin people. Edward Dorn, *The Shoshoneans: The People of the Basin-Plateau* (New York, 1966), is useful as a broader view of the simple culture of these people. Deward E. Walker, *Conflict and Schism in Nez Perce Acculturation* (Pullman, Wash., 1968), analyzes the processes of cultural change under reservation conditions.

The Southwest

Edward P. Dozier, *The Pueblo Indians of North America* (New York, 1970), is the most succinct and useful introduction to the complex cultures and historical background of all the Pueblo Indians. Laura Thompson, *Culture in Crisis: A Study of the Hopi Indians* (1950; reprint, New York, 1972), gives a detailed view of the past and present situation of a single Pueblo group. The standard introduction to the largest American Indian tribe is Clyde Kluckhohn and Dorothea Leighton, *The Navaho* (1946; reprint, Cambridge, Mass., 1974), which should be supplemented with David F. Aberle, *The Peyote Religion among the Navajo* (Chicago, 1966). Lesser-known peoples of the Southwest are the Yuman-speaking Pai tribes described in Henry F. Dobyns and Robert C. Euler, *Wauba Yuma's People: The Comparative Socio-Political Structure of the Pai Indians of Arizona* (Prescott, Ariz., 1970), and the Piman-speaking Papagos treated in Alice Joseph, Rosamond B. Spicer, and Jane Chesky, *The Desert People: A Study of the Papago Indians* (Chicago, 1949). The literature on the Apaches, especially on their 19th-century warfare with whites, is very extensive, but there is no general introduction to all the Apache groups or their present situation. Morris E. Opler, *An Apache Life Way: The Economic, Social and Religious Institutions of the Chiricahua Indians* (1941; reprint, New York, 1965), is a useful starting point.

California

The best brief introduction to the past and present of the many Indians of California is J.F. Downs, "California," in E.B. Leacock and N.O. Lurie, eds., *North American Indians in Historical Perspective* (New York, 1971). Two publications that give some understanding of the processes at work in the decimation of the California Indians are J.H. Bushnell, "From American Indian to Indian American: The Changing Identity of the Hupa," *American Anthropologist* 70 (1968): 1108–1116; and "The Cahuilla," in Wendell H Oswalt, *This Land Was Theirs* (New York, 1973). Theodora T Kroeber, *Ishi in Two Worlds: A Biography of the Last Wild Indian in North America* (Berkeley, Calif., 1961) is also useful.

The Northwest

Homer G. Barnett, *Indian Shakers: A Messianic Cult of the Pacific Northwest* (1957; reprint, Carbondale, Ill., 1972), gives an introduction to the situation of all Indians of the Northwest Coast. One of the best studies of a single tribe in this region is Elizabeth Colson, *The Makah Indians: A Study of an Indian Tribe in Modern Amer-*

ican Society (1953; reprint, New York, 1971). Theodore Stern, *The Klamath Tribe: A People and Their Reservation* (Seattle, 1965), is an excellent tribal account, as is D. French, "Wasco-Wishram," in E.H. Spicer, ed., *Perspectives in American Indian Culture Change* (Chicago, 1962).

Alaska

For the coastal Indians of Alaska, "The Tlingit: Salmon Fishermen of the Northwest," in Wendell H. Oswalt, *This Land Was Theirs* (New York, 1973), is a good short introduction. It may be supplemented with Philip Drucker, *The Native Brotherhoods: Modern Intertribal Organizations of the Northwest* (Washington, D.C., 1958), and Fredericka de Laguna, *The Story of a Tlingit Community* (Washington, D.C., 1960). For the inland Athapaskan-speaking peoples, James W. Van Stone, *Athapaskan Adaptations: Hunters and Fishermen of the Subarctic Forests* (Chicago, 1974), is a useful introduction.

Urban Indians

No general survey of the urban Indians brings the situation beyond the mid-1970s. Useful as an introduction is the brief treatment in Murray Wax, *Indian Americans: Unity and Diversity* (Englewood Cliffs, N.J., 1971). The articles in Jack O. Waddell and O. Michael Watson, eds., *The American Indian in Urban Society* (Boston, 1971), provide a somewhat uneven survey through the 1960s. Joan Ablon, "Relocated American Indians in the San Francisco Bay Area: Social Interaction and Indian Identity," in *Native Americans Today: Sociological Perspectives*, compiled by Howard M. Bahr, Bruce A. Chadwick, and Robert C. Day (New York, 1972), an early survey, gives the best-integrated view of Indians in one city. An excellent study of the role of pan-Indianism in urban Indian life is James Hirabayashi, William Willard, and Luis Kemnitzer, "Pan-Indianism in the Urban Setting," in Thomas Weaver and Douglas White, eds., *The Anthropology of Urban Environments* (Washington, D.C., 1972). A useful short demographic study is Henry F. Dobyns, Richard W. Stoffle, and Kristine Joes, "Native American Urbanization and Socio-Economic Integration in the Southwestern United States," *Ethnohistory* 22 (Spring 1975): 155–179.

Federal Policy toward American Indians

Of the two most comprehensive accounts of American Indian policy, the one by S. Lyman Tyler, *A History of Indian Policy* (Washington, D.C., 1973), is written from a government administrator's point of view; it includes useful lists of sources, especially for published and unpublished government documents. D'Arcy McNickle, *Native American Tribalism: Indian Survivals and Renewals* (New York, 1973), analyzes policy from an Indian point of view and is more selective. Different phases of policy development are described in two books by F.P. Prucha, *American Indian Policy in the Formative Years: The Indian Trade and Intercourse Acts, 1790–1834* (Lincoln, Nebr., 1970), and *Americanizing the American Indian: Writings by the "Friends of the Indian," 1880–1900* (Cambridge, Mass., 1973). See also Loring B. Priest, *Uncle Sam's Stepchildren: The Reformation of United States Indian Policy, 1865–1887* (1942; reprint, New York, 1969).